T0381439

THE
PASSAGE
TO
WISDOM

Discovering the Secret Life of the Heart

KIM DU PREEZ, PhD

BALBOA.PRESS
A DIVISION OF HAY HOUSE

This book is a work of non-fiction. Unless otherwise noted, the author and the publisher make no explicit guarantees as to the accuracy of the information contained in this book and in some cases, names of people and places have been altered to protect their privacy.

Balboa Press books may be ordered through booksellers or by contacting:

Balboa Press
A Division of Hay House
1663 Liberty Drive
Bloomington, IN 47403
www.balboapress.com
844-682-1282

The author of this book does not dispense medical advice or prescribe the use of any technique as a form of treatment for physical, emotional, or medical problems without the advice of a physician, either directly or indirectly. The intent of the author is only to offer information of a general nature to help you in your quest for emotional and spiritual well-being. In the event you use any of the information in this book for yourself, which is your constitutional right, the author and the publisher assume no responsibility for your actions.

Any people depicted in stock imagery provided by Getty Images are models, and such images are being used for illustrative purposes only. Certain stock imagery © Getty Images.

Author Photo by Estie du Plessis of Winelands Photography

Print information available on the last page.

ISBN: 978-1-9822-5959-4 (sc)
ISBN: 978-1-9822-5958-7 (hc)
ISBN: 978-1-9822-5960-0 (e)

Library of Congress Control Number: 2020923434

Balboa Press rev. date: 12/07/2020

My love.

This is from you, with you,
and for you.

Forever and beyond.

Contents

The Tools of Wisdom: Prerequisites of Path

Gifts of the Heart: Rewards of Path

Preface

The mornings belonged to us. Before we entered the world, my late husband and I would sit in the stillness and make that day count by capturing the wisdom we were learning. From March 2011, we wrote a short "thought of the day," and over the years, we accumulated hundreds of these little bits of wisdom, poetry, and other pieces of writing.

After his sudden and unexpected death in January 2017, I decided to put these thoughts in an order. Doing this was a labor of love and the only thing that gave me a sense of peace and relief from the pain of my devastated life and shattered heart.

I used a well-known qualitative research method called "grounded theory," which I had previously used in my PhD, to categorize the thoughts into themes. From there, a process began to emerge, and the themes took on a life of their own.

The work was painstaking and paradoxically took me directly into my emotional pain while simultaneously healing it too. Most days, doing this work would simply make me cry. It was intensely painful and beautiful and freeing.

Sometimes we are given wisdom, and we have to grow into the understanding of it. I have spent the past several years understanding this wisdom and how it relates to living our lives, walking our paths, surviving the stresses and strains of daily life, and fulfilling our reasons for being.

You may read this book in any way you prefer. Although it is a "thought of the day" format, it is not about a thought for the day. It is about all the thinking that became this day. The thought only gives us a moment of inspiration, a moment of reflection, but it then requires the thinking process to make that thought part of every day. Every thought may be well considered, but it remains meaningless unless understood. And understanding that thought, understanding that thinking, needs a constant interaction with our souls and the wisdom it brings.

As a side note, I use the words *head/mind* and *heart* interchangeably with *soul* and *ego*, and while they are technically different, using them this way allows for ease of reading.

This work is by no means expertise; it is simply my understanding, which holds so much meaning for me. It is the light in my darkness. It is my sincere hope, however, that it holds some value for you too.

Acknowledgments

When you are thrown into stormy seas, God always throws you a life jacket—or a few. For me, this has been you, Leo Hibbert. How would I have survived the past few years without you? It just doesn't feel possible. Thank you for your invaluable thoughts on this book and for helping me stay afloat in my endless and overwhelming sea of grief.

My dear friends Paul and Marjoleine Coetsee who have been my rocks, spiritually and practically. Your prayers for me and my children and your solid, consistent friendship have been the stable ground that I have stood on for the past few years. You were the divinely chosen instruments in one of our greatest gifts of all: our precious son, Cameron. Mo, you sang for us at Thinus's funeral and dropped everything to help pack up my house and move me when I was really sick and needed help but couldn't ask. Your many acts of love will go into my Love Album and will be treasured for all time.

To my tribe, my family. There are some bonds that endure all things and withstand the many trials of time and life. You have stood by my side through all my valleys and mountaintops. Your unfailing presence and support through my life make me understand that the bonds that exist between us are not mortal but are divinely ordered and extend way past this lifetime. We are a heavenly tribe too. My mother, Lucile Keet, your love never fails, and my siblings—Gary Knoetze, Bridget Fourie, and Claire Mallon—you are the golden thread that runs through my life. I have never extended my hand without one or all of you holding it. My late dad, Joe Bischoff, you are most certainly enriching heaven with your loving and witty presence.

My late husband, Thinus du Preez, and my children—Cameron and Morgan du Preez—you are my heart. You have taught me what love really is. Thinus, you walked me straight to my soul and have been my greatest teacher. You, my love, have been the hero of my life's story and the enabler of my biggest and most precious soul dreams. You always said that it was your destiny to bring me to mine. What is that if not the greatest act of self-forgetfulness and love? You three are my love for all eternity.

To God and the host of heavenly beings that have guided my journey. Without you, I am nothing. With you, all things are possible. How great thou art!

Introduction

For it is in you,
the secret passages of your mind,
that you store the wisdom
that you cannot find.

It's in the growth of your soul
that you reflect
some egotistical goals.

It's in the passage of time
that you have learned
the reality of your mind.

It's through forgetfulness
that you have discovered
the true stillness.

It's in the wisdom,
the beauty of your inner self
that you will reveal tomorrow's secret,
for yourself.

It's in showing others that you will learn
to forget your past
and live through the guidance of your heart,
and not your mind.

The Passage of Discovery

Find Your Path by Finding Yourself

Discover Your Programming: The Discovery Quest

It's not just about the discoveries
we make in this world.
It's about the discovery
of ourselves in this world.

We are forever focused on discovering
the new and the exciting,
the history, the beauty, and the pain
in this world we live in.

We embark on journeys to find the highest peaks,
the most beautiful spots, and the most important places
to fulfill this need to accumulate the knowledge,
to discover what's out there.

We must turn to ourselves
and start to discover inward,
finding our peaks, our beautiful spots,
and our places of importance.

It's through that understanding
that we will find a message from our souls,
guiding us to discover everything
of real value in this world.

Discovery brings with it wisdom,
for when we know more,
we understand the answers
to the questions that are with us.

January 1

"Don't let yesterday make tomorrow wait."

The process of discovery, of getting to know oneself, is not just about the trappings of one's past. It's more about the purpose of one's future. We often live through yesterday's eyes, with fear and anxiety and all the experiences that formed us into who we are. It's these trappings that often stop tomorrow from happening because it's difficult to let go and accept the purpose and the trust we need. Instead of seeing the world through yesterday's eyes, we need to find today's vision for tomorrow; that will unlock our futures. And when we stand in amazement of its beauty, we realize that our pasts can never be allowed to direct our futures—except through the knowledge and wisdom we have gained.

January 2

*"Become all you were created to become—and
not all you were programmed to become."*

We limit ourselves by becoming our programming. We stop short of evolving and becoming what we were created to be. It is important that we see the difference and that we live with no ceiling and allow our souls to show us the path. When we believe in our paths, we realize that nothing happens by chance. We are created to become all our destinies require. Our biggest limitations are all the programming we have allowed to influence our destined outcomes. We are what we have been created to become. We are not what we think we have been programmed to be.

January 3

"What we learned yesterday makes us grow tomorrow."

We live our lives understanding our pasts and living them in the future because we cannot embark on a mission of growth unless we shed the baggage of our pasts. Our programming needs to free us, not keep us locked in fear. As we understand, we unlock, and as we unlock, we climb and grow, because we know that our programming is ready to grow with us. So, as we tackle every obstacle, we follow the trust and obedience that made us understand our pasts, and we bring that clarity to our minds. And this clarity frees us from bondage to this world because it allows our wisdom to teach—and it brings happiness and joy to this world.

January 4

"The essence of our purposes is all about programming."

When we look at our purposes—the meaning of our lives, our paths, and our destinies—we realize it all relates to how we are programmed, how we change that programming, and how we program others. Our purposes are therefore all about programming and the choices we make, the influences we seek, the guidance we accept, and in turn, the ways we influence others and change their programming. The lessons we learn guide us on our paths and secure insight and knowledge that, if applied correctly, radiate wisdom that other souls lap up as their programming. We must therefore understand the significance of programming in our purposes because it affects our paths, and if we program correctly, the paths of countless others.

January 5

*"To really trust, we must overcome
this world's programming."*

Throughout our lives, we are programmed not to trust. We are programmed in the negative. We are programmed to expect the worst. This world programs us not to grow and to remain stuck in the endless circle of self-doubt. That programming teaches us to question our reasons for being here. It is important that we understand that when we program others, we reflect our own programming. It is therefore imperative that positive programming shows opportunity, shows growth, and shows that everything is possible because we trust and are following our purposes. When we program, we must program through confidence because that brings confidence. The biggest lesson in trust is patience, but the biggest lesson in growth is discovery, and for that, we require confidence, belief in our abilities, and the deepest sense of understanding that we are on the right path and that all will end well. The programming of this world shouts catastrophe; it preaches fear and anxiety. The programming we require shouts possibility, preaches confidence and peace, and makes every day the joy that it is meant to be.

January 6

*"Walking through the passages of our pasts
makes us understand our futures."*

Connecting with our histories, with our pasts, creates the evolution we require to grow into the future. The wrongs, the good paths, and the ability to grow all help us understand our futures. It is through the junctions of our histories that we determine our courses of action. They are the direction boards that lead us in soulful ways. Often, we must go back and touch them to unlock the doors to our futures. The most important aspect in walking through the passages of our pasts is the reminder of forgetfulness. The past reminds us that growth is a constant, and reflection on our histories gives insight. It should not burden us; it should free us. Walking through the passages of our pasts makes us appreciate the beauty of the here and now.

January 7

"It is through discovery that we gain a new appreciation for life's potential."

This world, our programming, and their influences trap us in fear and limit what we see in life. When we find our connections, we start lifting the lid on our preconceptions and how our programming and our fears hold us hostage. They limit our potential. It is when we understand our growth that we discover life has even more potential than we ever thought possible. The discovery process is a freeing experience that makes life a beautiful journey.

January 8

"Memories are clear and unobstructed
when seen from our souls."

Don't let your ego obstruct your view. Don't let your ego stop you from being grateful. Forgetfulness means forgetting what the ego needs and wants and remembering what the soul requires. Our souls see memories as lessons of joy and sadness, of growth, and of where we come from and how we will go forward. Memories should never be obstructed through the fear the ego brings; we should always try to show and to lead the way we want these memories to grow in our lives. We must understand that they are part of our discovery, not to be held onto but to be understood and then to be let go. We must see our memories clearly, and that can only be done through the eyes of our souls.

"Discovery is not about what we want to discover.
It's about what we need to discover."

When we get our egos to muster up the courage to follow our souls, when we make that connection between our heads and our hearts, our discovery process starts. Our egos will always show us what we want to discover; they will try to reflect on our achievements and not our lessons. It's during these processes of learning that we must remember to discover what we need because discovery is about growing, about evolution, and about purpose. We must always ensure that whoever starts discovering purpose will discover the ego's wants first, but we need perseverance to discover our needs.

"Let memories be moments of soulfulness."

When our souls are full, when our imaginations are clear, and when we are filled with love—those are our moments that must become memories. Those moments create the programming that makes us function on our paths with our souls leading the way through access to our memories of the past. Memories are programming that either needs correction or makes us lead lives of joy, fulfillment, and destiny. Memories that are not made from the soul and need correction are part of the discovery process of correcting our programming from the past. As we program others, it is important that we program memories that are moments of soulfulness because they become the programming of the future.

*"Overcoming the past determines
the way we face the future."*

Growth comes from the lessons and experience we gain through our lives, and it is made up of choices and decisions that affect our egos and our souls in different ways. How we face the future, how our egos face the future, is hidden in the way we have resolved our pasts. Decisions and choices that bring fear and anxiety allow our egos to reign supreme. To overwhelm the soul's quest for answers, we need to face the future. Our pasts determine the way we interact with this world and the way we find the reasons for our actions. We must therefore always be clear about our discoveries. We must be clear to understand our pasts. And we must allow our souls to heal the wounds and set our egos free from fear and anxiety because answers can only be given when we trust our souls to be the true guides they are.

January 12

*"Bad memories are just memories. Don't
mistake them for programming."*

It's so easy for us to fall back on our programs of the past because
they give us safety. We must identify what are merely memories
rather than making those memories part of our ongoing
behaviors. We keep reacting to those memories rather than living
in the moment. Memories are events, occurrences, and processes
that happened in our lives and have one of two purposes: a
lesson or programming. Good memories are about programming
because they come from the right place. You have to be extremely
selective in your choices: which do you take forward and how?
Do you take it as a memory or as programming? How do you
react to that lesson—and how do you integrate that lesson into
your life? Don't see the devil in every rose.

*"Don't change your canvas. Change the
way you look at your canvas."*

When we discover, when we grow in understanding, we shouldn't change our environments or our canvases, but we should change our eyes—the way we look at our environments and at our canvases. We must see different colors, and we must embark on painting with different strokes, filling the blank spaces with knowledge, wisdom, and an intense ability to grow. We cannot throw away our canvases. We cannot ignore our canvases. They carry our wisdom. They are the reflections of what we have been and of what we will become. Don't try to change them. Learn from them. Changing them is wasting energy and time, but looking at them with newfound wisdom brings positive changes to the way we see them—and not judgments.

January 14

*"Positive thoughts lead to positive
programming and enlightens the way."*

We must search our selves, our hearts, and our souls; we must question and test our anxious thoughts for it is there that we find the detours off our paths. With the variety of detours available, it is difficult to stay clear and focused on one's destiny. It calls for searching for those positive thoughts, which breeds positive programming and straightens our way.

January 15

"Use the moments with others in discovering ourselves."

During our walks through life, the biggest opportunities to learn, grow, and connect with ourselves is through the interactions with everyone around us. Other souls— no matter how deep or shallow, how connected or not—give us opportunities to discover more and more about ourselves. Every moment we have with others opens up a small window of opportunity where either the soul or the ego can slip through and grab that moment in discovery. It is therefore important that we allow these moments to be guided by our souls so that our discoveries can be lessons and not just egotistical trips. So, use our moments with others to learn more about ourselves.

January 16

"Moments become memories because
of what they program."

We all know that not every moment is turned into a memory, but we clearly understand that certain moments become everlasting memories. These are the moments that we must treasure because they come directly from God to guide us on our paths. Some memories come from negative moments, but over time, we should see the lessons in them. It is important through our awareness that we create moments that program positive memories. Life is made up of events that guide us on our paths to fulfill the purposes we came here for. Some moments are not seen, felt, or understood for years after they have become memories. This is the awareness, the understanding, that we must teach about. This lack of awareness to see the significance in moments makes our lives troublesome, anxious, and void of purpose. So, from now on, be aware of the moments that program our memories.

January 17

"Do we correct our pasts or do we just forget?"

When yesterday still influences today, we must be aware that what happened in the past, what happened yesterday, needs addressing and needs change. It influences what happens today. When we live through the regret of yesterday, we cannot accept the bounty that is there in the future because we carry this ball that drags and slows us down. How do we correct if we don't accept that yesterday is causing harm to today? And so we grow.

January 18

"When you are in a rose garden,
why focus on the thorns?"

I n an anxiety-ridden, fear-driven world, we often focus on the wrong things. Changing one's programming and renewing one's character calls for our souls to focus—and not our egos. We often make the changes but fall back on old habits because of years of programming, relentless trust issues, and defensiveness that make the ego strong. So, when you are in a rose garden, see the roses, their colors, and their beauty. And somehow, the thorns will fade into the background.

"We are programmed for our tasks."

Deep within our souls, we are wired to do and fulfill the purposes we were given. We have the ability, but through life and through the programming of life, we seem to unprogram our deepest sense of purpose. Life's programming builds obstacles, forms fear, and makes us lose the essential programming we have. So, are we programmed by life to reinforce the programming of our souls? Or are we programmed to disregard the programming of our souls? It is these teachings that we must understand and convey. For programming of the world must reinforce the programming of the soul and not contradict it. We are programmed to succeed. We unprogram ourselves to fail.

Discover Your Ego:
Your Barriers to Wisdom

A passage to wisdom is never a given.
It requires sacrifice, it requires understanding,
and it requires trust.

Our whole lives often lead to such discoveries
and with all the turns and obstacles we create,
we obstruct this passage, we build walls,
and attempt to withhold our purposes
from our souls' wisdom.

But as we learn to understand our hearts' purpose,
we let go of what obstructed
and what closed this passage to wisdom.

It is not that you are punished,
it is not that you are stopped from growing,
it is not because of a lack of understanding,
but it's all about the complexity of being ready.

So, as we grow through life
and as we embark on a new adventure,
so we carry with us that baggage of our pasts.

Now a passage to wisdom carries one question, and that is:
does my baggage obstruct or does my baggage assist
in finding this passage to wisdom?

For the more we learn, the more exhausted we become
and the more exhausted we become,
the more we must learn to turn inward
and focus on our souls' wisdom.

For the busier we are, the quieter we need to be.
For when the storms are raging,
the clearer we need to see.

So, turn inward
and find that comfort
and the quiet faith of knowing.

January 20

"Spiritual growth requires an effective ego."

To grow spiritually means that our awareness is elevated to a level that understands our purposes. Often we live for this awareness, forgetting that our egotistical effectiveness is as much a component of our connectedness, and it is this well-balanced synergy that stimulates our growth. We can't grow spiritually if our egos sabotage, do not accept responsibility, or withdraw from the world and the functions required. Spiritual growth needs freedom to express and to nurture, and that must be created through the effective ego. An effective ego makes way for the soul to grow. It creates space, it accepts responsibility, and it fights for the spiritual purpose of the soul.

January 21

*"What your ego tells you about life says more
about your ego than about your life."*

When we discover that the voice in our heads is not us, but that we are the one that hears it, we start to find true growth. When we distinguish between the ego's grandeur creating the fears and keeping us prisoner through our programming and a lack of wisdom, we can discover that there is the soul: the voice we must listen to that is different, that knows the way, and that we must follow with trust. Wisdom comes from our souls, and it will tell us everything about our lives because we must trust and allow ourselves the silence to hear what we should without the ego's interruptions. Build the strong connection because that is where we find the difference that brings us meaning.

January 22

"Our ego's biggest strength is the burden of our pasts."

Time brings a heaviness, a weight, to our shoulders. Our egos entrap our lives with the weight of time, and they constantly remind us of the burdens we carry from the past. Because of that, they trap us with fear and hold us in anxiety. We can only escape and lighten the load through understanding and trust. For what the future holds evolves through discovery. And when our souls replace the burdens we carry with the trust that what tomorrow brings was decided through our choices today. Destiny is part and parcel of time. It reveals the wisdom we have gained and reflects a shedding of a wrong burden we had to carry.

January 23

"We create the emptiness we feel. We create the void that we search to fill."

Being grateful comes from having a positive mind because it reflects our souls' position in our lives. The ego drives us to fill the emptiness with all the problems and with everything that brings fear. And so, the emptiness grows. When we go in search of perfection, perfection as the ego knows, we will find the obstacles and encounter the barriers, and our emptiness will grow. When we look at the beauty of a rose, every petal isn't perfect, yet it shows its beauty through that imperfection. Our lives are about fulfilling a purpose. And through all the joys and troubles, we will grow, in finding the meaning to fulfill our reasons for being. Our emptiness is not through a lack of ambition or an egotistical endeavor. Our emptiness grows through a lack of understanding and always searching for what is better, what is perfect, and ignoring what must be done to the present. We must complete before we can move on.

January 24

"Don't let your ego's thirst drain your soul of its power."

The ego will forever search and will forever create the barriers, the fear, and the anxiety that drive us to thirst for more. Of worldly opinion, possessions full of emptiness, and the loneliness of importance. Don't let your ego encircle your life through competitive games; instead, allow your soul to create the riches that fill your life. The wisdom of your heart needs no importance. It exists to show you the beauty of your way. Let us not enclose our souls' purpose through chasing what our egos make us fear.

January 25

*"Changing your conditions on the outside
doesn't change the conditions on the inside."*

No matter how hard the ego tries, it will never be able to give us the peace and security that our souls are destined to give us. No matter how we try to change everything around us, we will not escape the fear and anxiety within us unless we find the trust and the purpose in our souls. The conditions within can only be ruled by the ego if we allow it. It brings doubt, fear, and anxiety because it needs control; therefore it imprisons us and limits our growth in fulfilling our purposes. Changing conditions only grows the soul when the soul allows the ego the space to connect and make the environment part of our purposes.

January 26

"Your ego's wanting is never cured by getting."

What the ego needs can never be satisfied in accumulating everything your ego seeks. What the ego wants is to find the connection and address the need to search with a knowledge and trust and wisdom of the soul. The ego's need is only there because of our programming, our pasts, our fear, and our constant anxiety to find direction, to find our paths. When we find our paths and grow in trust, we realize that the wanting is not cured by getting. The wanting is changed by giving.

"Don't meddle with your experiences."

I t's the ego's nature to control our experiences, our existence. Awareness means being aware. The biggest obstacle must be the ego's conflict between acceptance and control. Don't meddle with your experiences. Accept them when they are right. Reject them when they are wrong. Trying to control them brings ideas and thoughts that lead to unhappiness. To be joyful and at peace requires accepting the experience for what it is.

"What the ego seeks on the outside the
soul can answer from the inside."

The ego's biggest illusion is to lead us in a way where we search for answers outside ourselves. It is the trick that brings fear and anxiety to control us. What is outside us are our dreams, but what is truly important are the dreams inside us. They are our purposes. On our journeys, we must remember that what is outside us can only have meaning if we answer it, if we understand it, from inside us. Our souls have the meaning.

January 29

"Don't let the ego trap the wealth of the soul."

The wealth that is locked up in the soul can only be exhibited when we allow the doors to be open to the world. The ego will always endeavor to trap, to hide, the soul's beauty and wealth. Control, fear, and egotistical importance are often used to conceal our inner beauty. Our negative thoughts, our fear, and our need for self-importance removes the wealth that our soul needs to spread. So, we need to find the trust that will allow our ego to remove the trappings and expose the wealth in our soul.

January 30

"Allow yourself to discover the meaning of life in others."

Our nature is often so problematic in seeing the true nature and beauty in others. Our egos lead like a sharp spear in discovering the meaning of life. And when our egos lead, they judge. They hurt. They don't listen. So, no meaning can be revealed through others. When our souls lead, they lead through embrace. They don't judge. They always listen. They seek the meaning of life in others, and in doing so, they fill all the potholes we have in our own discovery of the meaning of life. If we lead with our souls, we will discover so much through others.

January 31

"Inner beauty is revealed when outer importance fades."

They say that less is more, and when it comes to our inner wisdom, that is very important. Our inner wisdom shines through when we remove the walls, the barriers, and the obstacles of our seemingly egotistical importance. We become more when our egos become less. We shine brighter when our egos fade. We understand more when the channel is directly to our souls and not obstructed by the layers of outer importance. Let our beauty be revealed through our souls' inner wisdom by making our importance less and our quality more.

February 1

"Your emotions are what fuels your ego."

The volatility of our emotions is what brings anxiety and fear to our egos. It brings the doubt, and it removes the trust. Emotions bring negativity and establish the way we look at everything around us. The control of our egos, therefore, rests in the stability of our emotions. Emotions bring doubt, yet our souls preach trust. We must find the path where trust brings the calmness to our emotional states, brings the joy to our negativity, and gives us the foundation that brings stability to our egos. We cannot live on emotional highs, but we can live on soulful trust. We need not rush. We need not pursue the emotional highs because they will soon be followed by the emotional lows. It is time that brings the wisdom through trust and faith to our emotional nature and makes us understand that the fuel of our lives is the connection between our souls and our egos. It is not the emotional rush.

"Never let the fear of falling keep you upright."

The world drives us for achievement and for growth, in an egotistical sense. We search for success, for prestige, and for the acknowledgment of all the egos around us. There is nothing wrong with that, but we must never allow the fear of falling from that pedestal to stop our growth, our purposes, of the real and magic moments of our souls. It's when we fear that we will fall in the world that we run too fast to stay ahead, to stay upright, and we lose the insight, the wisdom, our souls project. Bring balance and understand that the fear of falling is not about growth; it's about the world.

February 3

"Pessimism is what stains our souls."

Being pessimistic fuels depression, and it robs us of the beauty of life. The soul's purpose can never be held ransom through the negative thoughts and ideas our egos conjure. Purpose must be the positive feedback we get through trust and living through the knowledge, the wisdom, of our souls. Pessimism destroys that trust, and it makes our purposes—how small or how big the element might be—a burden in our lives.

February 4

"Can faith ever overcome control?"

Can the pessimist in us have faith? Can the gloom prophet relinquish control? The biggest obstacle we face is finding a way to do the work and have more faith than control. It is important that we do the work, but it is just as important that we do it through faith and not control. Fear and anxiety breed control, and ultimate control is to transfer fear, to create more anxiety through the way we act. We judge, and we instill patterns in our environments that force us into fear and through that more control. Can the pessimist in us overcome control and accept faith? This can only be done through the understanding of the connectedness between our heads and our hearts. Control is not a safety net; it is a barrier to a happy and fulfilling path.

February 5

"What we see in others matters less
than what we see in ourselves."

Insight is developed. It is never a given, but it sure is needed. To become guiltless is to find that wisdom that allows us to shed that guilt and not allow it to form the basis of every fear and every trouble we encounter. That guilt fills us with anxiety and stops us from truly moving on. We need its justification, and we seek it in others. We search for blame, and we dig through our nonsensical and egotistical behaviors to make us feel better—or so we think. If we can blame, we don't have to look at ourselves. We don't have to address the guilt. And most importantly, we don't have to listen to our souls. What we see in ourselves takes time to understand, but it's more important than anything we see in others and try to understand.

February 6

"The mind is filled with clutter and empty boxes."

Through control, we think we are organized. We think we have packed and structured in a way that gives us the security we need. We believe it brings an absence of fear. Through our organizational skills, we focus on control. We fill our minds with clutter, and we collect empty boxes to prove how much control we have over our souls. It is through this clutter, this organizational control that we lose the freedom that comes from our souls. The need for control can only be described as a fear for the trust we should have in our souls. We must discover that when we let go of control, we do not lose the organizational focus or the structured approach. All we lose is an obsession to do it in a way through our minds. True guidance is going in search for the best way and finding our souls' guidance through the trust—and not through the importance of our minds' or our egos' control. When we clear our minds of clutter and focus on our souls' presence, we can remove and can throw away all the empty boxes, find the space to believe and find faith, and discover the trust that guides us through our souls.

"Why must everything have a reason?"

We are programmed to search for a reason in every event, every emotion, and every thought. The more we grow up with fear, the more profound this need to find a reason in everything around us. For that's the ego's way to protect. It explains and brings comfort, or so we think, to our existence. There must be a reason when we are happy. There must be a reason when we are sad. It can't just be to find joy or to bring thought. The reason must be profound and explainable from this world. It can't just be our souls nudging us to understand. It must be explainable through our minds. We conjure up reasons for everything around us—for everything we touch—but often all that is needed is to enjoy the happiness, to think through the sadness, and to remember the trust that is with us through our souls.

February 8

"Where there is fear, there is also a need."

The ego will always create fear and anxiety to remove us from trust. It is important that we understand this, we understand the fear, and we associate it with a need. This need might be a direction post to our paths. It might be a hidden wisdom to understand our purposes. It might be the signboard to evolution. It is important to find the connection and deal with the need on our paths. When we embark on a road of trust, we soon find that the irrational fears subside and are replaced with firm belief and confidence in what we are doing. When we address the need, we will find that our egos surrender the fear.

Discover Your Soul: Your True Self

The magic of life is locked up
in the discovery of our paths.
For that is where our uniqueness lies.
That is what we are destined for.

Yet as we go into this world
we are programmed to fear,
when we should be programmed to discover.

It's then that our uniqueness fades
and we are filled with anxiety
in finding our way.

We carry this baggage of programming of the past
that destroys our uniqueness
and makes us less mindful,
and through that, absolutely lost.

For we must remember
to forget ourselves to discover our paths.
So, when we talk about this uniqueness,
we must remember to nurture it well.

For we are created with difference,
and that is the strength that makes sure
that we are fit for our paths.

And it's when we realize that that difference
is God's way of showing our uniqueness,
that fear turns to confidence
and we forget ourselves
and we remember our hearts
and we fill this world with the wisdom
that we will find in the magic of our paths.

So never allow uniqueness to become a weakness.
Never allow difference to bring fear.
But show the way by leading with the heart.
For it's then that happiness fills our minds
and joy flows from our mouths.

So, remember that to be unique
is a strength given to all,
but discovered by only a few.

February 9

"Remember who you are."

During our lives here, we are tempered by our programming, fear, and anxiety. They force us to build walls and obstacles to protect what our egos deem important. Now that is not all of who we are. Who we are is found in that innermost cavity where our souls see beauty and love controls everything. It is in that inner sanctity that you will understand your purpose and your path. It is very important to sit down and access your self as often as possible. Access your true self—and not your egotistical self.

February 10

"Let your true self be found."

No one can find you unless you want to be found. No one can discover you unless you want to be discovered. It is our lack of understanding that makes us hide behind walls of ego, while peeping through little gaps, seeing the beauty of our souls, but stopping its revelation. Listening intently will reveal the inner self. At that point, we must allow ourselves to discover that we only need to be our true selves in order to reflect our purposes. Listen intently because when you do, you will hear the message coming from within. And that will allow others to find you.

February 11

*"The emerald in your soul is the
knowledge it has of you."*

The soul's true beauty is the knowledge, the understanding, of our purposes and our paths. It is this value that we must be ever aware of. We must strive to unlock the communication, to delve into the treasure chest of lessons learned and experiences gained. We must remember the feeling, the awareness, the insight, we experience when we access our souls' treasures. It brings joy, and an abundant exhilaration that supports our knowledge that we are doing the right thing. The emerald in our souls can only shine through when we remove the layers of disbelief and egotistical fears that bring the anxiety and cloud the beauty of our souls.

"Why wait a lifetime to reveal your character? Start discovering it today."

We are programmed to trust in fear because trusting in faith requires letting go of control. How can we find the pinnacle of existence if we live in trusting fear, to stop us and hold us hostage to the demands and egotistical anxieties of this world? When we trust, we let go of fear, and we live as one, with soul and ego combined, connected through its common purpose of wisdom. We find our true character when we let go of all that covers it to discover our true self and a meaning for our existence. That discovery can be a plotted path of lessons learned, but trust reveals our true character, and for that, we must understand that love and acceptance bring trust and overcome fear to make our existence purposeful and kind.

February 13

"Feel the warmth inside you. Yes, that warmth, that's the real you."

We are spiritually connected in a pure and vibrant way. It's a warmth that radiates to us and shows who we really are. We disguise this with the ego building high walls to hide this warmth and cover it with anxiety, fear, and restlessness that obstruct connectivity with ourselves. So, we need to go and, in solitude, find this warmth and acknowledge it as the true inner self—and then find ways to show it. When the ego blocks, we need to look for this warmth inside. That is the escape, and that's how we break the obstructions and barriers the ego presents. So, find that warmth, that light, and hold onto it because that is the real you.

February 14

"True beauty in life is the basis of
inner character: the soul."

We must make sure that what we reflect comes from within—and what is within is our inner character, our soul. This connection is made when we find intimacy with ourselves and discover peace, harmony, and a true balance, knowing what we reflect is who we truly are. It's when we find that balance that we discover the true fruits of life, and it has its meaning in serving a greater good rather than the egocentric obsessions of our worldly ways. True beauty is therefore not something we can attach to ourselves; it's something already with us that we must first discover and then reflect upon. These are the curbstones of our paths and will keep us strolling to our destinies without obstacles.

February 15

"Don't plant a tree and forget to water it."

Our journey through life allows us to discover all the hidden talents we have been blessed with. Each time we discover a new talent, it's like planting a tree, but planting these trees requires the commitment and the understanding from us. That we must nurture it, we must take care of it, we must give it time, and we must allow it to grow strong in its own confidence. For as we water it, and as we prune it, it will develop into the tree of purpose. Bearing its fruit and giving shade. Bringing the comfort when we find doubt. Bringing the warmth when we feel cold. These trees, our talents, are the anchors to our souls. For they point us in the direction of our paths and hold us strong on this journey. Nurture them. For they are our true blessings.

February 16

"Let your values come from your soul, and then they will not be easily influenced by the opinions of others."

O ur egos can build up defenses of fears and anxieties based on events during our lives or our programming. It is through forgetfulness of oneself that we have to walk the path around these egotistical defenses to discover the values in our souls. In discovering these values, we soon learn that they can't be influenced or changed. They are based and founded on our intrinsic soulful purpose that stems from our relationships with God. These values should build our character, form our reputations, and be the essence of our programming. Everything should always start from our souls' value opinion and circle outward to find answers.

February 17

"Treasure and grow your true assets."

When we think of the beauty in people, we often see their success, their kind ways, and their wisdom. And when we see that, we long for assets like that. We must realize that all of us have true assets. It is often hidden on our paths, and as we grow, we discover them. Our assets are all the small attributes that our souls will use to make this a better experience and leave at a higher level through the lessons where experience is gained. All our assets are grown through experiences, correct programming, and discovery. They are true to us, we know them, and they are shown in our imaginations and our dreams. They come naturally, and they become us. The biggest obstacles to the growth of our assets are fear, anxiety, and self-doubt. That's why it is essential to find them, treasure them, and grow them.

*"Is our value defined by what we are
not—or what we truly are?"*

Acknowledging strength in others is a way of strengthening yourself because we all have our unique values, and they are defined by our purposes, our paths. Fear and anxiety rob us of the consistency we need to have value. Our value cannot be defined by others; it can only be defined by our purposes. When we live with meaning, we will find that we have value in most things we do. However, it is that search—that acceptance, that fundamental understanding, that one aspect—brings us more value and defines us in the world. That is where our souls and our egos meet in a strong connection that displays wisdom, free of the fear and anxiety that this world brings.

February 19

"Everything has a pattern, including us."

We must live life through the discovery and understanding of our patterns, designed to fulfill our purposes. When we are in conflict, when we live against our patterns, and when we break our molds, our purposes, the obstacles emerge and become insurmountable. By renewing our minds, our egos, the patterns of our souls emerge. Walking against our patterns brings heartache and sadness. Renewing our minds and seeing our patterns brings flow, joy, and fulfillment. Our quest to understand this pattern makes us understand the real life we love.

February 20

"Let your talents be your compass."

nside us, where our souls meet our egos, there is a bond that brings the talent we have to the forefront. It displays our abilities; it forges all the possibilities. The talents we have cannot be found in others. We must develop them because we know them, and they are ours. Let these talents become a compass to guide us to our purposes and lead us in a way that fulfills and helps others on their paths.

February 21

"I belong to myself."

There is a freedom in belonging to yourself. It means that you know your soul, and you belong, you exist, because of it. Understanding that your life is filled with joy brings the need for an oasis of spirit. Belonging to yourself requires that you replenish and build the strength through your soul, convincing your ego that who you are is who your soul says you should be. You belong to no one—except to the destined path that your soul has ownership of. Return to your oasis and replenish your strength. For that makes belonging understood and life joyous.

The Passage of Connection

The Bridge to Wisdom

The Gap:
Connect Your Head and Heart

It's the tussle between our heads and our hearts
that makes this journey difficult.
For we always want to follow want we think we need,
when we need to follow what we know is right.

It requires a certain awareness,
a certain forgetfulness of our own self-importance
to bridge this gap between the head and the heart.
For what we know in our souls
must be the cornerstone of our existence.

And to lead the way remembering what is right
needs a forgetfulness of our egos.
For to forget the importance of this world
ensures that we remember the importance of our paths.

Every day, we must build this bridge.
For the stronger we get,
the stronger the bridge,
and the wiser we become to all its obstacles.

*"The gap between our egos and our
souls is the cause of our pain."*

The ego creates expectations. It seeks importance and relies on fear and anxiety to determine our headings. It requires control, and it brings us closer to not understanding and not fulfilling our true purposes. This wrong path causes pain and suffering. Our souls bring our dreams, our purposes, to reality. It knows tomorrow, and it needs to show us—through all the growth and lessons—the right way to our destinies. The gap between the ego's expectation and our souls' reality needs to be closed. For the wider it becomes, the more the pain and suffering.

"Let our egos be the mirrors of our souls."

The true connection between our souls and our egos must be understood and seen in the ways we act. Where there is low connectivity, our egos display true chaos because that is what reigns. As our connections with our souls deepen, our egos become the mirrors that reflect the beauty of our paths and therefore of us. It is important that we always accept that we must act through the connectivity of our souls and our egos because the closer they become, the more meaningful our lives and purposes become. So, allow our egos to be the mirror of our souls, and every moment will be a discovery of purpose, path, and destiny.

February 24

"When your soul is open, you experience love.
When your ego is open, you experience fear."

I t's difficult to understand that we have to live in the moment with awareness and thought because the past has gone—and the future is unknown. It is therefore important that we understand the balance between our souls and our egos. When the connection between them becomes strong, we find an equilibrium where awareness of the moment is more important than any thought of fear or any deed of just love. We evaluate and are able to respond in accordance with what the moment dictates. It is the only connection that removes the obstacles since it makes our paths very clear. When our souls lead, the equilibrium is easily found because it opens us to love and understanding. Open our hearts and open our minds. Not in isolation, but in combination.

February 25

"We need a guard dog that is also a guide dog."

The ego needs a guard to stop it from roaming free. To stop it from instilling fear. We need a guard to block us from the egotistical and the superficial, but we also need a guide to lead us. To show our egos the way. Without it, it is aimless—and it will search for excitement that causes pain. It will preach fear that brings harm. It will turn frustration into anger. We must erect a guardhouse where our guard dog can keep a vigil and lead the ego with our guide dog to grow. It's not about protection; it's about connection. Allowing our souls to guard and to guide brings us the fulfillment, the prosperity, and the emotional security we deserve.

February 26

*"Our soul's light always shines—but how
clear is determined by our head."*

Leadership is a way of life. It is the ability to confidently follow our beliefs and trust in our purposes. When we lead from our souls, our egos submit to and follow our purposes as the light that emanates from the soul clearly shows the path. The only way we can dim that powerful light is by making our center of control, our leadership HQ, our heads. When we follow the ego's self-importance, the light from our souls becomes a dim candle with no effect and little direction on our paths. It becomes a constant struggle to wrestle control away from the ego, and we often lose this fight in fear and anxiety. Now when the light shines brightly, we accept the leadership of our souls. And to make the light shine brightly, we must tell the ego to stand down, to listen to the soft inner voice of reason, because that is the collective effort of all the wisdom that has come together to guide us on our paths. This light is so clear; it need not be front and center, but somehow, it glows for everyone to see. Let our souls shine and allow our heads to follow because that makes trust, love, and happiness the guiding forces in our lives.

"Always try to understand because there will
always be time for judgment later."

The soul grows through lessons that allow the ego to become more connected. Our souls will always try to understand, but the ego will always jump to judgment because it defends its worldly view, brings importance, and focuses our lives on the world. Our souls seek to understand, to bring the ego closer, and to make the connection stronger. So, when we live in this world, we must seek to understand through the soul and don't always jump to judgment through the ego.

"Let your soul express who you are through you being."

The connection between our souls and our egos can only be seen when we act in ways that exhibit our purposes and our destinies. We have to show through our ego's actions that our souls are in control. Expressing who we are is as much about understanding our purposes as it is in the way we act in the world. The connection between our heads and our hearts needs the balance to allow our souls the opportunity to express who we are, and in doing so, allow our egos the freedom of being exactly what we are.

March 1

*"Let the wisdom you have provide
the confidence you need."*

We always find that we drain our confidence through fear and the inability to understand. We try to control and create that confidence. We try through egotistical errors to make ourselves confident, but that is all in vain. Confidence is only as strong as we allow our connection between our souls and our egos to be. The more we grow, the more we nurture that partnership—and the more confident we become as we are walking on our paths. Our souls understand and will provide all the understanding, all the knowledge, and all the confidence we require. Do not build up confidence through egotistical ways. They create fear and take away the soulful confidence we require. The wisdom we have been given must become the source of our confidence. Because then we live from within.

March 2

"Your soul is the eternal optimist because
anything else has no future."

Connected understanding and wisdom flow from our souls when we allow them to. Our souls are the optimists in us. The soul sees the future, and it knows the purpose. The ego counters that strength by creating fear, negativity, doubt, and overall anxiety. Being optimists, our souls connect with this world through positive energy. The soul sees the possible and not the impossible. It guides us to greener fields, and it understands that faith, belief, and trust are its biggest allies. Optimism is what guides us. Allow our souls the freedom to be optimistic. Allow our souls to have that strong connection with our egos. For that brings the positiveness to light.

"It's not what you are seeing, or what you are thinking,
but where you are seeing or thinking from."

n a life well lived, we often find that the center of being was on the inside. For when we live through the ego, we make the outside important; therefore, we see everything as important as the ego deems it to be. The answers can only be found on the inside. For when our souls see, think, listen, and direct us, we find a positive force that guides us and our egos into seeing and thinking in a way that is purposeful to our lives. So, it is not what we see, but where we see it from.

March 4

"Build on your soul's energy because that is what grows tomorrow."

The dreams in our souls awaken us to our purposes. We must build on these dreams; we must dive into the well of energy that our souls provide. For that energy has longevity because it has purpose. The ego's energy is short-lived. It seeks short-term highs and creates long-term fears. It doesn't build; it brings anxiety. So, find the soul's energy, and with it, comes the quiet confidence of trust.

March 5

"Don't absorb through the mind.
Absorb through your heart."

We must remember that wisdom connects from within. It connects the simple but true facts of our daily existence. What it sees reflects not what we hear, but what we need to learn. When we intellectualize, we respond to this connection without accepting the message from our souls. There is a place for the mind, and there is a place for the heart, but whatever we do, we must allow the heart to filter the mind. For that protects the path and brings wisdom to our decisions.

March 6

"Courage comes from the soul. Bravado is the ego."

Never confuse the two. For courage displays the wisdom of our souls. It leads through trust. It finds the understanding that is required in any situation. Bravado, on the other hand, is the ego's way of defending our programming, our pasts, our fears, and the anxiety that makes grandstanding far easier than discovering. Bravado limits as it questions everything. It stops us growing, and it allows the ego the strength and position in our lives that bring bravado to the forefront. Courage allows our souls to act and set aside the fears our egos bring to stop us from following our paths. Courage is filled with trust, knowing that whatever the outcome, it is the right outcome.

March 7

"Moments only last as long as we want them to last."

Moments of joy, moments of anger, and moments of sadness are all emotions driven either by our souls or our egos. We determine how much value we give them, how long we hang on to them, and how they determine our actions every day. Moments have value when they connect us, when they make things clearer, when they spread the love, and when they seek understanding. However, moments can also be destructive when they cause obstacles or sit in judgment. We determine how long a moment will last. So, allow the souls' moments to last long and the ego's moments to be short and few; that is the path to joy and comfort.

March 8

*"Inner balance brings the joy and
peace that makes us grow."*

The tightrope of life requires balance. We find this inside ourselves. It's the connection between our hearts and our heads. Our souls and our egos. When we are in balance, we find joy and peacefulness, but when there is too much ego, or too much soul, we drift away from equilibrium and find unhappiness and a restlessness that slows our growth. We must never try to only grow in one of the two spheres. That makes us misunderstood, and it removes the peacefulness we need. Growing the balance in our lives is growing ourselves.

*"Let the courage of our souls guide
the impatience of our egos."*

We live in a world where enough never seems to be enough. The ego is riddled with imperfections and fears that we will not conquer and control our paths. The impatience of our egos never allows us to see the beauty we have been given in the moment. The impatience of our egos drives us to want more, need more, conquer more, and possess more, but we forget about the gratitude and courage we need to show for what we have. The soul only needs the knowledge and the wisdom from above to guide us to our purposes and to our destinies. It will fight, and it will win, and it will overcome the impatience, the fear, and the anxiety our egos deliver. All it needs is the wisdom that we know that often in moments we need to be quiet, we need to be still, we need to be thankful for what we have, and overcome the impatience for what we think we need. For then our purposes will become clear.

March 10

"Reward yourself, and the world,
with the logic of your soul."

The logic of our minds often renders our souls ineffective. For the science of the world cannot reason about the logic hidden in our souls. Our spirits drive the wisdom that comes directly from within and grows over time. This is not a logic of our minds, but it requires trust. The logic of our souls rewards us through our purposes, and it leads us to a destiny far beyond the logic of our minds.

March 11

"To be effective in life, one must love in harmony."

The effectiveness of our souls is reflected in the love they project. Our souls are the basis of leadership in our lives. It forms the underlying value in what we do and in what we want to do. It is, and will always be, the secret to our purposes. When we want to be effective, we need to ensure that our egos love in the same way. The ego needs to adjust and understand the purpose of our lives. It needs to see our paths clearly, and it needs to subject itself to the effective love given to the world by our souls. When our egos and our souls love in harmony, we find that our living becomes a stream of joy, an effective way of fulfilling our purposes. Because what we do does not only bring us joy but is the fulfillment of our destinies. Effectiveness is the harmonious junction of our souls and our egos.

March 12

"Improvement or enjoyment, similar but yet so different."

If the world was just seductive—or just about challenges—there would be no choices. Yet the valley between our souls and our egos exists because our souls want to improve the world, and our egos just want to enjoy the world. The balance, the connection, between improvement and enjoyment is the path to our purposes. It's when we find the bridge that connects our souls and our egos that improvement becomes enjoyment, and enjoyment ensures improvement.

Build Your Bridge:
Establish Your Listening Post

How do we escape the frenetic pace of this world?
Where we are driven through our egos
to find a way that brings the security
and quells the fear?

We find that when we are alone with our thoughts,
it's our thoughts that are driven.
It is our egos and everything in this world
that make us alone for they isolate us.
For all we see is the here and now
and the fear through our egotistical needs.

When we alone with our thoughts
we need not be alone.
For when we listen to the whisper,
the quiet voice of our souls,
it speaks of patience
it tells us where confidence is found
and our trust becomes the light to our paths.

And how we overcome obstacles
through listening well,
through understanding our hearts,
and making our souls a lamp to our feet
and a messenger for tomorrow.

It is when we are alone with our thoughts
that we should not stay
where ego in this world is at play.

But we should become silent
and find the voice of our souls
and listen to that harmony,
that peacefulness.

For that rejuvenates
and brings energy to our task,
and our daily growth.

March 13

"The faster we walk, the slower our progress."

t is in the stillness, a quiet seclusion, the peaceful and tranquil loneliness that we discover the highest mountains and the most beautiful valleys. The more we run, the more frenetic we become, the more we go on detours. In our inner rooms, we discover the answers and the meaning of what's to come. The faster we walk, the more we run, the less we give ourselves the opportunity to discover the real answer, the real meaning of what is to come. So, hold back, and find the quiet contemplation. When we become still, we are given and we find what is so obvious but yet so distant.

March 14

"Have a cup of tea with yourself today."

In this rushed world we live in, we often neglect the most important and give attention to the least important. We must always understand that our relationships here must be both horizontal with those around us and vertical with ourselves and those above us. And both of these call for time to contemplate on your own with thoughts and dreams that describe the essence of that bridge that connects your head to your heart. If you don't allow those moments of contemplation to be frequent and intense, you allow either the soul or the ego to focus your entire being without connecting. It is in those moments of contemplation that you allow your soul to describe to your ego the dreams, the path, and the destiny. And in the same way, you allow your ego to catch up and forget about all the things that seem important but are not. So, the essence of every day must be the time you spend having a cup of tea with yourself.

March 15

"Fear and anxiety are just the absence of understanding."

When we think, we must be careful not to make every thought the problem, the fear, that our souls need to overcome. We must allow our souls their clear paths. We must allow our souls clear access to explain and direct our thoughts to become the positive forces that our purposes require. Thoughts create the fear and anxiety that our egos depend on. For it is because of the lack of understanding that the ego always triumphs. It's only when we become still, when we become silent, that we realize that understanding comes from within. We cannot think it out or reason and debate it. It comes from faith and the internal knowledge of our souls' wisdom that wants to fulfill our purposes. Understanding crushes fear. It crushes anxiety, but we need faith to find understanding. We need silence to hear and to listen to the wisdom from the soul that delivers the peace and makes understanding real.

March 16

"Protect your heart because it is the fountain of life."

Like a fountain produces clear and sweet water, so our hearts provide for positive thoughts, a purpose-driven existence, and a life that is guided by love and not by chaos. Our hearts are the source of thoughts when we allow them the freedom to connect openly. Do not let the ego bring negativity and stop our hearts from producing the thoughts that should guide our lives. Let our hearts be the source of our thoughts. Protect them because they will always produce the clear and sweet water our lives need.

March 17

*"It's the absence of thought that reflects
the existence of wisdom."*

t is in the search of thoughts that we can hear nothing in
silence. When we ponder the ego's brilliance, we forget the
soul's wisdom. We must not be mistaken to think that thought
has no place, but to really understand our purposes, we mustn't
push or pull our thoughts. We should become silent and wait for
wisdom to be delivered. Wisdom has timing that is beyond our
understanding. Thoughts have no timing because they are created
in our heads—often with little regard for our hearts.

March 18

"Remember a book filled with beautiful images."

Our hearts set the course. Our heads require convincing and need to be forced to trust and somehow understand that the course set by our hearts is the right one. We must fill our books with beautiful pictures, remembrances of soulful events that turned our lives. This book is our meditation quest. It requires thought, preparation, and awareness because these images are what we require to stay connected. This book is filled with our dreams, it has our thoughts, and we are able to return to it and find meaning on our paths. Fill your book with beautiful images. For that gives us the silence we need to connect.

"Forget the day, forget the importance of the world today, and let's remember everything the world makes us forget every day."

t is not often that we give ourselves time to reflect and ponder on that which is free, beautiful, and not worldly. We have been given a promise, but we never trust. Nature survives through the trust and faith and love of God, and we can too if we escape the anxiety and fear our egos give us. It must be said that life is about balance, but how often do we forget the world and remember life?

March 20

"It is in the absence of thought that we learn the most."

Our preconceptions are often the biggest barriers to growth. They hinder our progress and stop the flow of wisdom the universe requires. Our biggest advances, our biggest growth moments, happen when we stop trying to be the teacher and remain the student. Thought, when generated through our egos, leads to fear and anxiety, and it builds the barriers that our souls need to overcome. When we enter with little or no preconceptions, accept the knowledge, the belief, that every moment delivers its own wisdom, we will soon find that when we speak and think, we deliver content from a different source.

March 21

"It is often the spontaneous thought that matters."

In quiet reluctance, we grow the most. It is when we are able to slow ourselves down, to not find the search for the opportunity to grow, that we grow. It is in the thoughts of tomorrow that yesterday makes itself known, and it is these thoughts that we need to correct. Our spontaneous thoughts come from the soul because they are not tainted by yesterday's actions. So, when your friend asks how to remove the clutter of anxiety from their life, you answer, "By rethinking yesterday's thoughts—only built on the clutter of anxiety." Listening to our spontaneous souls makes tomorrow a brighter day. The ego will always overthink, overcalculate, and overcontrol. Be still—for that is when the spontaneous thought appears.

March 22

"Sometimes you have to stop trying to succeed."

Trying too hard is often the obstacle that our egos use to exert control. We try to find the answers, we try to understand the problems, and through all that, we lose the insight that we were given. Passion is not something we are born with. It is something that is developed. And when we find that we are trying too hard, we lose that passion and the reason for creating and accessing our purposes. We have to sit back because insight and reason are often on the opposite sides of the scale. It's in the quiet times when we are not trying that we often find insight, and that changes the way we reason, but when we keep on trying, we never stand back to allow that insight, that passion to ignite the flame that lights up the way.

March 23

"Start every day with your heart—
and not with your head."

We must remember to set the tone because every day starts with our hearts. When our souls reinforce our purposes, our egos find value in the tasks of that day. When we awaken with our heads, we come alive with fear and anxiety, and we breed insecurity. Come alive with our hearts, and we focus our insides that will reflect our outsides. Purpose comes through our hearts, but it is executed through our heads. So, awaken every day through our hearts, and soon our heads will rest peacefully.

March 24

"Always recover by listening to your soul."

Our sensitive souls must be seen as the guiding lights in our lives. The soul is the listening post where we find our wisdom, where we find guidance, and where we understand our paths. When we go through the troughs and valleys of life and need recovery, it is important to find the quiet times and tune in to our listening posts to be given the energy, the wisdom, to recover and get ready for the journey ahead. We must understand that lessons are an essential part of growth, and as we grow, we often find we need to recover from the pain of lessons learned. It is in these times that our souls must become dominant. Often, the opposite is true as our egos establish control because we think we need protection, but recovery is about love. It is about the sensitive whispering of our souls to our egos that makes the connection stronger and allows us the patience, the strength, and the wisdom to recover.

March 25

"Moments pass, but it is the thinking that lasts."

All we are is but a thought. We act, we see, we feel, and we understand through process of thought. The most difficult of all thoughts must be not to think, to clear the passages of the brain and to be filled with the clarity of your existence. We know thought determines your next actions, but where the oneness of you becomes clearly evident is through the feeling and the connection with God. We think with yesterday's thoughts, and we apply with yesterday's actions. It is important that we understand yesterday's thinking because that determines today's action. As we teach, we must show that yesterday's thinking had a reason—be it good or be it bad—but to understand tomorrow's action, we must clear our minds of the thoughts about tomorrow and start thinking about understanding the thoughts of yesterday. We are but a thought. Nothing happens without thinking. It is the thought that makes us scared. It's the thought that creates anxiety. It's a thought that makes us angry, but it is also a thought that brings us joy, fills our lives with soulful content, and brings comfort. Start thinking about clearing the mind because it is in those moments that we discover our true thinking.

March 26

"Your heart never shouts; it only whispers."

t's the ego's bravado that shouts control and enforces fear. It overpowers the soft whisperings of your soul. It is very important that we know this because then we can recognize when our hearts are whispering softly. We can listen and grow accordingly. It is one of the great teachings that we come to understand and recognize the whisperings of our souls. We must learn because that brings us to our purposes.

March 27

"It is the noise in silence that we fear the most."

We often want to become quiet and connect with ourselves, but it is the noise of our egos that obstructs the clear voices of our souls. It is the clutter of control, of thoughts and fears, that makes silence an impossible event. Silence is not about thinking; it is more about listening. So, escape the noise in silence by emptying the head of thoughts and opening up to listen.

March 28

"Listen, and you will hear."

I t is the noise of the world that brings confusion. Through all the clutter, through all the noise, we will hear what we need to hear. And what we need to hear must be defined by our sources of direction. The world will forever tell us what we need not hear, but as we grow in awareness, we find the wisdom to understand the right message from all the noise. So, listen, and you will hear.

*"It's through our own silence that we
create silence around us."*

Stillness brings stillness. Awareness nurtures awareness. It is important that we relax into silence to allow our souls the freedom to communicate and interact with everything around us. The energy we attract comes from the energy we give off. When our egos lead the way, we find that silence in ourselves and around us has no place. When we recover to stillness, our souls will bring the silence to everything around us. And we will find our awareness to hear everything we require to make the silence the loudest message for all to see.

March 30

"Are you listening to yourself—or to others?"

We must be mindful that we listen to our souls and not to the pressures of the world we find ourselves in. When we listen to our self, we will hear the guidance we need to build purposeful paths. When we listen to others, when we listen to egos, including our own, we fill ourselves with anxiety. And every task becomes the search for perfection and not for meaning. Performance becomes everything, and growth—yes, the growth we need—slows down. Guidance has a clear voice, but we must learn to quiet the world down, enabling us to listen to our self.

March 31

"Develop your inner ear because that brings wisdom."

When we hear the sound in a voice, our egos are listening. It makes us alert. It awakens us to danger. The ego protects and listens to warn us of danger. When we listen with our souls, our inner ears, we don't hear the sounds in a voice, but it understands that listening brings wisdom. Not through what we hear, but through identifying its origin. The inner ear will guide us to hear the worldly sounds and distinguish them from the wisdom messages. We must develop our inner ear through awareness. Creating that listening post is the guide to revealing everything to the world.

April 1

"Escape from yourself today."

Use the moments and become a child again. Seek the pleasure that makes you escape your ego today. Find those relaxing moments that make you remember the joy of life. Find the happiness in a moment that leaves the stress and fear of your ego behind. Escape your ego today, and it will revitalize your soul tomorrow.

April 2

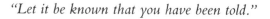

"Let it be known that you have been told."

How often do we ignore the message—the voice that brings us to reason—that explains our paths? How often do we follow our own convictions for the need of control or our own importance? How often do we ignore our own wisdom for the sake of others and their opinions? How often do we find ourselves lost because we do not listen or cannot hear? Let it be known that you have been told.

April 3

*"Every day needs a morning that
gives answers and peace."*

We must allow for quiet contemplation to give us a new sunrise each and every day. It is in these times when we become quiet and focused that we discover the answers we so often need. This sunrise becomes a dedicated time that brings peace and clarity to a day that is often filled with everything but soulful peace. We must allow time in every day to discover our sunrise and make our answers the facts that lead us on our paths.

*"Sit in silence and identify the things that are
bigger, more important, than yourself."*

We need the quiet times. Silent moments allow our souls the freedom to express what we need. These silent times bring us closer to understanding our purposes and our paths. When we sit in quiet isolation, we must identify what is bigger and more important. How we treat loved ones. How we understand our role in giving back. The way we help those less privileged to find tomorrow. How we develop souls from young to old. The way we see ourselves. The part we play in this bigger cause. It is important that we identify the bigger things because they will remain the pillars that we anchor ourselves to in delivering our destinies. We must never be bigger and better than the pillars we find in our lives. If we don't learn, we slowly die and drain ourselves of wisdom. Identify the bigger things.

"Make time in your life for afternoon tea."

Your life must be lived. It must never be seen as a quiz in search of answers. For when we grow, we live. We walk a guided path. Where answers happen. Where time brings wisdom. Where readiness is not given but must be achieved. It's like afternoon tea, where it is somehow less about the tea or the afternoon and more about the time we spend in silence and understanding. Afternoon tea is not about talking or listening; it is about the quiet peaceful time that allows the universe to cleanse us from anxiety and fear. Because it shows us the beauty and joy in our presence. Whatever your afternoon tea is, ensure you do it often. For life must be lived.

April 6

"Meditation is not about discovering answers to the
world; it's about discovering answers for yourself."

The more we grow, the clearer we understand the meaning and purpose of our tasks. When we realize that our souls' growth is our ultimate strength, we stop focusing on the obsessions of our minds. Thee more our souls grow, the stronger our minds become. Our purposes unlock that freedom. So, when we find quiet time, when we bring ourselves to meditation, don't expect the revelations to obstacles in the world—expect the guidance for our hearts.

"There is always encouragement in voices."

No matter what, no matter where, no matter how, and no matter by whom, the spoken word must always be judged not from where we come from, but from where we are going. We must always endeavor to find the encouragement, to listen, to learn, to accept, and to forget. We must recognize our voice within. It stops us and swirls us around to face our paths, our purposes, and our destinies. Voices are the signposts that direct us; therefore, our ability and our insight in listening to them must become evident, clear, and important. There is always encouragement in a voice.

April 8

"It is truly an art to listen."

What the ego hears is not the same as what our souls see. What our egos hear is not the whispers of the soul's wisdom. So, in a crowd of voices, do we hear the ego's cries—or do we listen for a soul's whisper? To listen well is to hear more than the voice, the sound, of another. To listen well is to place that voice, that sound, with the whisper of their soul's wisdom. When we find that, we truly discover how to listen— and to listen well.

April 9

"It's in an absence of noise that we hear the most."

Our daily lives are filled with everything that we require to live in a useful way—but very little that we require to live in a joyful way. When we allow the noise of our daily lives to subside, we hear the beauty of our true life. Noise that is brought about by our egos contesting our places of existence and importance silences the voice of joy and destiny. We must therefore strive for synergy to create that strong connection between our souls and our egos, and in doing so, we will be able to listen to all the noises, be they egotistical or leading voices to our destinies. It is this positive conspiracy that allows us to grow and understand that noise can lead us or stop us, but we can only really, truly understand it when we become quiet and listen to the noise that leads. That only happens in the absence of worldly noises.

April 10

"There is a listening post tucked away. It's only you
that can hear it and reveal what it hides away."

We must listen with our heads but hear with our hearts. For what it reveals, we discover, we enjoy, and we make our journeys filled with joy and peacefulness. Like scattered sheep, we find these messages hidden in clouds and behind rocks. We pull them together; we form a picture. For that reveals the clarity we need to fulfill this purpose. Like scattered sheep, we find these messages, and they become a flock, all directed to form the basis of our hearts. It's the voice of our souls, and we need to hear it clearly. Not through scattered messages, but collectively, we must hear. So, find that listening post that is tucked away—and let it reveal everything it hides away.

The Passage
of Evolution

Walking Your Path

The First Connection:
Embark on the Journey of the Heart

It's remarkable how far we must walk
and how long it takes to cover the ground that we need
to understand the beginning.

For it's only when we get to the beginning
that we are ready to start this race
of developing the wisdom within
and confronting our paths
beyond what we know is possible.

So, as we walk this road
we must always remember that it starts,
not because we want it to be the answers we need,
but we start this road because we don't understand
the meaning of our lives.

And the complexity to grow is therefore hidden
in our lack of knowledge and wisdom.
It's only when we get to that point, the beginning,
that we realize that the strength of connection
makes walking this path far clearer,
therefore, far easier.

We have to stand back often
and allow the wisdom to lead us
and not the knowledge in our minds,
but to be guided by the trust in our hearts.

"Let your journey begin—no map required."

The journey of the heart will always encircle the mind. For the path to fulfillment leads through intellectuality and finds depth in the journey and not so much in its perceived destination. Never let the journey of the mind overshadow the travels of the heart. For when we see the beauty of the soul, we gather the wisdom designed to lead us to fulfillment. Let the journey of the heart find the trust, the wisdom, and conquer the circles of our minds.

April 12

"The longest journey is from the head to the heart."

n the journey of life, we must always follow our purposes. They are purposes we find through the lessons we encounter. This growth brings us to our destinies, but often we find that the obstacles in our way obstruct a clear and direct way. We have to find the long way around. For if our egos and souls are not connected, we make our paths very difficult to see. So, the longest journey for most people is to find that first connection. It is a journey filled with insecurity, with fear, and with anxiety that only our heads can cause. The longest journey must be walked with the soul leading the way. The longest journey is to connect our hearts to our heads, and to do that, we will discover trust and allow our vulnerability to remove the obstacles we encounter.

*"To connect with the world, you must
first connect with yourself."*

I n this world, we often want to change things, make them better, and understand them more, but before we can do any of that, we must fulfill that ever-long yearning we have to connect with ourselves. In connecting with ourselves, we bring the wisdom and the understanding that make the world easier to understand. Connecting to ourselves is like a set of new glasses, and we see the world through different lenses. The connection we have with ourselves is what we need to connect with the world.

April 14

"Build strong connections through discovery."

The first question you must always ask is the quest about connectivity—where are we heading and what are we destined for? These connections can only be made and strengthened through a process of discovery. The question must be related to the connection required for our destinies, so it is imperative that we ask in discovering where we come from and what our programming is. Each discovery process must be riddled with imagination because clues, thoughts, and moments of a beckoning destiny are hidden in them. When we allow ourselves to escape into our souls and connect with soft images of our beckoning destinies, we are walking the road of discovery and making connections that will lead us to our points of joy. Building these connections must always start with a question of what and how strong, if at all, our connection is with ourselves, therefore our souls. This connection is the first step in resolving our quest to find our paths. It builds the bridge to our destinies. So, build connections through discovery because they are everlasting and answer all the questions we require to find our points of joy.

April 15

*"Trust is established through the partnership
between our souls and our egos."*

We must accept that our souls know the answers. They understand our paths, and they want to show us our purposes. So, when we trust, we allow our souls the freedom to guide us, to show us the way, to grow us, and to establish the wisdom that makes us glow from within. This world, on the other hand, forces our egos into fear, into doubting our souls, into anxiety, and into a loss of trust because we doubt our own abilities. The stronger the partnership between our souls and our egos, the more we will glow, the less we will doubt, and the more we will do. Not because we control through fear and egotistical ambition, but because we allow our souls the freedom to act in confidence. Trust grows through this partnership, and we must learn to block the negative influences from this world on our egos that make us doubt and follow the answers we find within.

April 16

"Reveal yourself first to yourself and then to others."

Our most complex task is finding separation between our heads and our hearts. It's a journey of awareness that leads us to understanding. As we follow this path, we reveal our souls' purpose, and we get to know our self and strengthen the connection with our egos through wisdom and experience. When we reveal ourselves, we find the answers. We understand the questions, but the most difficult part must be separation. When do we act through soul? When do we act through ego? This can only be understood through the process of revelation. As we move closer and the circle becomes smaller, our understanding, our wisdom, will teach others the objective views of soulful purpose and not egotistical banter.

April 17

"Your eyes see what your head reflects."

We must always remember that we feel and act and encourage the energy that we see. It is thus important that we know where that energy comes from. If we allow ourselves to see only what the ego shows us, we will live in an egotistical, fearful, and anxious manner. If we allow our souls to reflect the positive energy around us, we will live in a creative and forceful manner on a path that is clear and aligned with our destinies. The connection between our egos and our souls is of the utmost importance, as this connection attracts, discovers, and reveals the energy around us that makes us see our paths toward our destinies. It is important that we know and understand what is reflected to us.

April 18

"Always remember that we are more spirit than flesh—we are more soul than we are ego."

Where we concentrate our efforts is where our direction leads. If we concentrate our efforts in worldly pettiness, that is what we become. We must always remember that we arrive in spirit and we depart in spirit, and what happens in between must be the luxury of learning lessons, of growing, and of understanding ourselves. Yet we transform this luxury into countless actions that cause us misery, hurt, and pain because we live in flesh and ego. We must always find direction through our spirit or our soul because that will allow us a bigger and better perspective on the pain and suffering that should transform us into better and more advanced in understanding ourselves. Always remember that we are more soul than ego.

*"It's only when you discover your heart
that you discover your head."*

Our minds are filled with countless thoughts and programming that creates all our fears and anxieties. It is the flint that causes the fire. The ego dominates through the mind, but as it goes, the head is often in total disarray, pulling you in all directions with no real path or destiny in sight. Our heart, on the other hand, is there long before the head, sees the path, and understands its destiny. So, when you discover your heart, a clear imprint will be made on your head—and that's what your ego will become.

April 20

"Searching for something to make us happy brings a lot of unhappiness."

t's the ego's misguided path to search for happiness in the world around us. It is a misguided understanding that being connected to the world will stop the anxiety, the fear, and bring identity to our being. Our souls know the path, and it requires the humbleness and forgetfulness of our egos to connect and to understand that the answer to happiness is already within us. Searching for it in objects outside creates more fear, heightens anxiety, and is a sure way to become miserable. First find connectedness to your soul—and then discover the happiness within.

April 21

"The only guide for your heart is your heart."

The soul cannot be guided through reason, intellect, or self-importance. We cannot force our souls to move in a way that we determine through thought and egocentric beliefs. The only guide to our soul is our soul. It is therefore important that we listen very carefully to guide our heads with our souls and not the other way around. Fear and anxiety contribute to us trying to lead our hearts and souls to what we believe is safety. Our souls and hearts know best and fit all decisions to our purposes and our paths.

*"It's not your life that is in a maze. It's
your mind that is in the maze."*

When we live through our hearts, there are not many turns or twists on our paths. For what there is brings us wisdom and guidance. When we live through our heads and minds, our egos will invent every possible turn and twist to make us into what we think we should be. It is our heads that need discovery through the maze; our hearts know the exact path.

"Are you anchored in your head or in your heart?"

n the memories of life, we must look back and—in understanding our growth—see when we were anchored in our heads and when we were anchored in our hearts. As the connection grows between our heads and our hearts, the anchor becomes a pivot that allows us strength of direction on our paths. When we are anchored in our hearts, our heads can never run away. They are securely fastened to our paths, to our purposes, and therefore to greatness. It is when this anchor is in our heads that we lose sight of our paths. We lose stability, and when rough seas hit, we run the risk of sinking or running aground. Always bring the anchor back to our hearts because our souls are our anchors in life.

April 24

"Don't let what is irrelevant obscure what is relevant."

It can be easy to focus on what we think are the important issues. Our egos will always drive us to what we fear or perceive to be a threat. This holds us in anxiety and prevents us from seeing and growing what is real. When our spirits, our souls, find the path and start the process of fulfilling their purposes, we cannot let what is irrelevant capture us and obstruct what is relevant.

April 25

"Reality is totally different from what
our egos show it to be."

The ego needs to build walls. It needs to remove our confidence. It needs to shatter our faith. For then it remains in control. It therefore distorts reality. It encourages fear. It boils up anxiety. For that gives it the control. We need to accept that our souls know best. That the path we walk will be guided if we believe and communicate directly with our true self. We must judge reality, not through the shadows of our egos, but through the clear vision of our souls.

April 26

"Let not what you know stop you from learning."

It is the preconceived idea, it's that judgment, that forms the barrier between grasping and understanding your future and missing your path. It is that knowledge that comes from the ego that stops us from exploring because it's the fear, the preconceived notion that I know this is not right. When we listen with our souls, we understand the signals and act on those signals, not through preconception, but through an understanding of positiveness toward the future. For the ego brings the negative, and it focuses on judgment. That is how it builds this barrier. What we know, what our egos know, can only be changed if we open ourselves up to learning more from our souls.

April 27

"Fulfillment is not found through achieving.
It is found through understanding."

The ego will forever chase the next quest to perceived fulfillment. We must remember that our whole defense, most of our programming, is based on our egotistical standing in this world. It's only when we connect to our souls that we find the answers of true fulfillment. It is not linked to who we are, our own importance, or the egotistical fears and anxieties we try to escape. Fulfillment is linked to our purposes, to an understanding of tomorrow, and the role we have in it.

April 28

"Is life an intimate journey or a crisis-filled bath?"

To identify confusion and lack of direction, we must evaluate our journeys to determine our connections. When a life is an intimate journey, it is filled with trust and finds balance between our soul and our ego. It allows us the peace and gives us the time to ponder and absorb the wisdom we have received. When we lack connection, the balance is disturbed, and we find that confusion reigns. We try to be all soul, but we actually remain all ego. The journey is riddled with obstacles, filled with crisis, and we have little time to absorb our wisdom. The secret is discovery, which brings us to a connection that answers the questions of our life's journey.

The Crossroads:
Choose Your Source

What changes your life?
What brings you to alter your course?
It's a question that can only be answered
through our discovery of wisdom.
For the more we discover, the more we know ourselves.

Through the growth of our lives
we encounter many crossroads.
Some will take us on a long detour,
yet others allow us to cross right into happiness and joy.
It's the decisions, the choices we make
at those crossroads that bring fulfillment or pain.

So, what changes do we make to alter our courses?
Our hearts will always be filled with a yearning,
and it's those pressure points that bring us to a place
where wisdom reveals the truth
and brings us to alter our courses.

It is listening to and understanding
those yearnings from our hearts
that make change possible.
For when we are quiet, we can hear them clearly.
But as the world goes, we shut those yearnings out
and fill ourselves with activity
to stop any changes from happening.

So, what do we need to change?

We need more of that quiet time so that we can listen.

We need to find those yearnings that will lead us to a place
where meaning and fulfillment
become our daily bread.

*"Know this: choosing the right path
is your responsibility."*

Everything is given to us to walk our paths. All we need is awareness and a growing understanding that will correct and reprogram our predetermined thoughts about which path we must follow. As we become whole and closer to ourselves, we often find that our growth and our lessons are all about the programming we have been given. Such programming often causes us to choose wrong, which leads us astray. It is therefore imperative that we instill awareness that will remove all the anxiousness created by programming, which will allow us to reprogram and learn the required lessons. This can happen several times over; the more we learn, the more aware we become. The more aware we become, the better our service to others. It is our responsibility to choose the right path and to learn, grow, and develop. It is not always the easiest path, but it is definitely the most rewarding one.

April 30

"Always choose to identify with your soul."

n life, we are confronted with choices about our paths, about our purposes, and about what we identify with. A strong connection between our soul and our ego will always ensure that we identify ourselves with our souls. It is when we identify ourselves with our egos that we lose clarity. We blur our purposes and confront the world with fear and an uneasiness that needs us to control everything. When we live life through identifying with our souls, we live in a purpose-driven way, understanding who we are and connecting ourselves with the world in a clear and transparent manner. When we teach, we have to show people a way to identify with their souls. That will open their paths for them.

May 1

"Wisdom is seldom revealed through the ego."

In life, decisions must be made on everyday events—and on fundamental issues regarding our destinies. It is important that we teach and show where our decision-central is. When our decision-central is in the connection between our heads and our hearts, wisdom flows and decisions are made from the correct place. Ego very rarely delivers wisdom. So, ensure that in the process of programming, we establish the connection early and clearly.

"We grow through what we feed ourselves."

The path we choose is highly dependent on the nourishment we receive. The teaching, the programming, will determine our choices. The food we feed ourselves—or the food we are being fed—brings clarity or cloudiness to our purposes. The better the nourishment, the clearer our understanding. Our egos react to the impulses, the food, around us, and only time will bring clarity to our choices from within. Make sure that as we grow, as we travel through time, that we teach the importance of seeking the food, the nourishment, that keeps our paths, our purposes, clear. For obstacles come from filling ourselves with an understanding that is not from within us—but is solely dependent on what is outside us.

May 3

"Why is the hole more attractive than the light?"

We seek the obstacles and the negative because we cannot trust the hope we find in the positive. When choices are made, we are attracted to the darkness because it seems easier to be the victim than the hero of our souls. Our ego lives with fear and creates anxiety; therefore, it seeks to shelter and hide our true abilities. We always move toward the hole because our egos convince us of its shelter. The light shines and needs our trust because it brings us in the clear where our souls reflect our purposes and our egos need to disappear. Don't allow the negative to reign supreme because that strengthens the wall of separation and stops our souls from being in control.

May 4

"Don't let the ego shut us down."

The ego brings forth all the bravado that we need to feel important in the moment. It lacks the ability to see a future and then drives us down the wrong path—in the knowledge that pleasure in the moment is more important than true joy in destiny. These momentary lapses in judgment must be identified as the ego's way of leading us, and in those moments, we must seek the courage of our souls in determining the difference between the ego's choice and the right choice. It is important that we judge this through our feelings from within because that is what will determine the right choice and our paths. The ego shuts us down through these momentary choices of pleasure that lead to pain, fear, and an uncontrollable anxiety; they stop our souls from acting through the service to ourselves and others. It is therefore important to see when the ego is attempting to shut us down and call on the courage from within to act decisively.

May 5

"We have already lived today—yesterday."

It is not what today brings because today is only a reflection of yesterday's choices. So, what we find in today, what we become aware of today, we decided about yesterday. So, as we go into every day, remember that the choices we make today, the decisions about tomorrow, make tomorrow happy and joyous or sad and regretful. When we program others through the actions of today, we must remember their impact in the future and live by our choices every day.

"What you want is relevant to what you have chosen."

We must understand that our lives are a process of growth. What we want—our souls' purpose—can have no meaning if we have not chosen it. What we choose is what our lives are about. When we build a strong connection, our choices are about growth, about learning, and about understanding our paths. It leads us to what we want. It creates a deep understanding of our purposes. Vision comes from what we want—and then we have to make choices that lead us there.

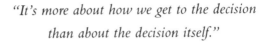

May 7

"It's more about how we get to the decision
than about the decision itself."

To lead from within requires the application of the programs and processes that reflect the connection between our souls and our egos. Decisions we make should be about our growth, our lessons, and not about the worldly views of popular choice. When it comes to daily decisions, it is more about how we make them than what they are. We must always find the wisdom that reflects the right choice because it shows the purpose of our souls. The process we follow must be guided, not through egotistical fear, but driven through a soulful purpose and the knowing of what tomorrow will bring. Growth can never be easy because then it is not growth. When we just receive, it means we were not guided and are not following the program of how we should decide. Gifts are direction boards to growth. Real growth is a gift from hard work. Our programs of choice must always be the ones that we find within—and that requires hard work.

"It's all up to us."

When we need water, it is all up to us when we get it. The food for our souls is determined by our choices in finding it. We can feed ourselves with everything that is wrong and obstructive to our destinies or decide to make the choice to feed ourselves with rich nourishment that leads us on a path to our destinies. Now these choices are as much about knowledge, awareness, and wisdom as they are about the reflection of the world we allow ourselves to live in. Impulsiveness and egotistical over-eagerness are often the source of malnutrition on spiritual journeys. We must accept that we are given all the resources, all the talents, to control that aspect of our journeys. Namely, we decide which food source we will use to nourish ourselves.

May 9

"Allow my soul to reflect all the beauty I live by."

What manifests in yourself must be seen from others' perspectives. What you allow to manifest in yourself—you can allow the ego or the soul—must be seen from other people's perspective. What you allow to shine through mirrors who governs your life. If you allow your ego to govern your life, that is the perspective that will be reflected to others. If you allow your soul to govern your life, that is what will be reflected to others. The reflection of your source is your decision about your path. That is the most difficult thing for humans to do because you lose the mask of the ego, the defensiveness, and you only find the strength from within when you allow the soul to reflect the beauty of you.

May 10

"Don't see yourself in others."

The greatest teaching is the understanding of separation. It is when we find the ability to walk our paths without our egos inflicting their values on others. It is when we make choices that show our purposes and not our pasts. It is when we make a decision because of the greater good of tomorrow's vision, and by definition, our destinies. We therefore can't see ourselves in others. For then we choose to make decisions that are not about tomorrow; they are about the ego's feelings, interpretations of life, and understanding of the past, imposed on that person at that time. We must teach separation—where our choices are made by our purposes and not by our egos—or how we will be seen or understood by the world. When we do that, we show the strength of our souls, and it's reflected through our leadership.

May 11

"The source of our dreams delivers our paths."

Everything in life revolves around our foundations, how strong they are, what they are made of, and how they evolve. This foundation becomes the source that will drive our paths toward our destinies. Now when we program, we must make sure to build the foundation on rock and create a source that delivers the path to find the destiny. When the source delivers the wrong path, corrective steps are filled with hurt, pain, and confusion, which leads to fear and anxiety. We have to identify the source, and we have to make it clear. Like a spring gives water, the source, our soul, delivers our paths.

"Fill the canvas that is your life with bright colors."

Discouragement, negative thoughts, and seeing the impossible are all the black and dark colors that our egos paint our lives with. It forms blotches of despair. It makes our lives seem troublesome and filled with chaos. It is a choice we make to either paint in shades of darkness or change and fill our lives with the blossoms of color that show our paths, our destinies, and ultimately our happiness for being here. Don't allow voices of discouragement and negative thoughts to fill your canvas with black. Rather, understand your faith that everything will be overcome in time and with hard work. Focus on your inner voice; it preaches the bright colors, the happiness, and the joy we share in this world.

The Growth:
Understand Your Lessons

There are no short journeys.
There are journeys that are wrong,
but there are no short journeys.
For every journey grows with us, and we grow with them.

So, when we take these journeys,
when we walk these paths that lead to fulfillment,
that force us to face awareness,
those journeys are never short.

For you are engaged, you are called,
to learn and be understood.
To find that awareness about yourself
to find that awareness about your soul
to awaken and discover your role.

That can never be a short journey.
That can never be a quick walk.
That is a long process of growing
and finding the wisdom that unlocks your soul.
To show its light, and fill this journey
with your presence and beauty.

So never think that this is a short journey
because your real journey is still to come.
This is a long journey
for it is one.

"To evolve is to transform into the
better version of ourselves."

Through growth, we follow a process of becoming wiser, of understanding and committing to our journey, here and beyond. If through that growth we don't become better, we don't become a higher version of ourselves, it means that our pasts had very little purpose. It means the obstacles and the mountains we climbed had only pain and no purpose. It means the programming and the discovery we encountered fueled only regret and very little progress. Through evolution, we transform by listening well and understanding the purpose of all our elements in the past. That is evolution, and that equips us to listen better, to program more, and to discover our true paths and what we are meant for.

May 14

"It requires the soul's sensitivity to
appreciate the lessons in life."

In a rushed existence, the ego reigns supreme. We miss the beauty in a smile, the forgetfulness in helping others, and the passion for our purposes. It requires a spiritual sensitivity to see this beauty and develop an awareness for the lessons we learn. It is a sensitivity that finds the beauty in obstacles as we understand the wisdom they create. These lessons are part of our function to overcome ourselves and impart the wisdom to others, making our lives as useful as intended.

"The purpose of experience is meaningful growth."

All the experience we gather must lead us to the lessons we require to stay on our paths and to grow to our destinies. Experience has an evolutionary purpose to guide us through a net of barriers and obstacles, knowing that we evolve with every step. Understanding the past and our experiences is the basis of this evolutionary growth, and that will lead us to become wiser and more meaningful in the ways we program others in their evolutionary processes. So, experience has a purpose, and it's all centered in growth.

May 16

"Seek opportunities to grow."

We must always be on the lookout and be aware of opportunities to further the quest of our souls. This awareness requires that we understand our purposes and seek to fulfill them through growing and understanding and remaining in service of others. If we don't seek opportunities to grow, we will find that events will be placed on our paths, forcing growth to enable us to understand our deeper purposes. Often, we don't see these opportunities and are unaware of the need to grow further. That is when our souls and our egos become distant from each other, and we find ourselves lost and circling in places where nothing benefits our paths. This search needs to end through becoming aware. That is when we will start looking for the right opportunities to grow.

*"Let your awareness reveal the summers in your
winters and the winters in your summers."*

The wisdom we have within will show us and will give us the appreciation to explore and understand our joys and our sorrows and our fears and our happiness. We must understand the roles these lessons have. For not all lessons are guided, but obstacles do act as signboards to purpose. So, when we find the joy or the sadness, we must be aware of their roles in our life processes.

"Our scars are our unique little wisdoms."

The scars we carry reflect the lessons we have learned, and in some great way, the wisdom we have acquired. We must make sure that these scars carry and reflect the wisdom they intended to acquire and are not just egotistical wounds with no meaning. So, when we find ourselves learning or trying to solve a lesson or hardship, we must always reflect on the fact that the scar that has been made is unique to us and will reflect a wisdom that is designed for us.

"Build on what we understand."

Life is filled with the complexity of the mind and spirit. There is so much we don't understand, but we must build on what we do understand. That is the revelation of that time. We need to strengthen that understanding because what was revealed leads us further to uncover more and to understand more as we grow. Fixation on perfection and what we don't understand weakens what we have and the purposes we have been given at that moment in time. Our energies are consumed by what we don't understand and what is not ready at the time. We need to hand that over and allow it to mature because patience also brings wisdom.

May 20

"Growth is progress in a backward way."

When we grow, we learn—and we find the understanding we require. When we teach, we need to illustrate that growth is progress, but that real growth is progress of knowledge already with us. When we grow on our paths, we grow in areas, in thoughts, and in processes that are already clear to our souls. When we grow in the wrong areas and step onto the wrong paths, our souls cannot assist with the true and complete understanding. Positive growth is growing in the things our souls already know. It is discovering the path to our destinies. So, true growth is progress in a backward way.

*"Your ego's growth comes through the
execution of your right dreams."*

When your ego finds the trust and follows the path that fulfills your destiny dreams, it is growing. It is a growth filled with trust that brings the heart and the head closer together. The growth of the ego is a balanced approach based on trust, surrender, and the understanding of what is required in the world. It is the combination that feeds confidence and leads us on our destined paths. Growing the ego is fulfilling our dreams in a soulful way.

*"Grow to achieve because it's when we
achieve that we really grow."*

Finding the talents that we have—exploring our greatest strengths—makes it clear what our purposes and destinies should be. It is through achievement that we find answers, either in pain or in joy, but it is through that achievement that we build the confidence that gives the freedom to create more, to achieve, and to understand the meaning of that achievement. For achievement with little meaning is an egotistical conquest to show importance. Achievement for growth and for spiritual value drives our purposes. It allows the soul to give back and to part with the wisdom. For that doesn't complicate; it educates. When we find that freedom in achievement, we understand its purpose.

*"The biggest growth should not be in your
flowers; it should be in your roots."*

As we grow in life, we mustn't just grow in ego—or in the outer being that we show the world. Our biggest growth must be in our roots. Where we come from, and where we are going, needs the nourishment, the food, that can only come from our roots. We must grow them to clear water, to soil filled with food because that will display the flower with the beauty it deserves. When we don't grow our roots, our flowers show beauty but little joy. It is only temporary. Lasting nourishment will not come from our roots if they are not grown. Strong roots mean we have altered our pasts and corrected our futures, and that becomes the basis for strong branches filled with beautiful flowers and fruits.

May 24

"We don't need a crisis to grow. Crises only stop us and ask us to grow."

We understand our lives to be filled with obstacles, with crises, and with difficulties. We don't need all that to grow. We can grow in silence if we follow the paths to our purposes. Obstacles and difficulties are only signs to stop or point us, to beg us, to listen, and to grow. We must teach others not to become martyrs of growth but understand that our problems are the road signs that give us direction. Grow through discovery, trust, and understanding for that is where wisdom is at its best.

*"Motivation to grow can never come
from frustration of thought."*

Frustration and the negative thoughts our egos create will always limit our potential to grow. Motivation, strength, and wisdom can never be born through the frustration we find ourselves caught in. The peace we search for is never outside us; it is in our eyes looking out. We must never allow frustration to disturb that peace or unsettle our tranquility because that limits our growth. It creates turmoil, and our egos search for conflicts. That is how fear and anxiety are fed. We must remember that motivation, strength, and wisdom are positive energy, and we must fight off the negative thoughts and the negative energies that try to disturb our growth.

"Look at the tall trees and see how slowly they grow."

Growth is not a process that is led by time; it is a process that is led by readiness. As we process all the lessons and all the events around us, we prepare ourselves and open ourselves up for growth. Now as the trees need water, nutrients, and sunlight to grow, we need love, insight, and a connectedness with our souls to grow. It is through the obstacles in life that we find the meaning of growth. Growth is never about time or about our egos. Growth comes from our souls.

"Perspective is an important element in growth."

The ego often focuses on the details. It ties us up in the process, in the past, in the elements that keep us bonded in today. Our paths though, our destinies, require that we have perspective, see the bigger picture, program accordingly, and understand that the details, the process, is a mere means to the end and not everything in between. It is therefore understandable that our wisdom, our insight, be required in every situation so that we have the perspective of tomorrow when dealing with today. Anxiety and fears are created for a moment and lack the understanding of tomorrow.

May 28

*"Settle in and accept because your
day is only just starting."*

You cannot change what you have to accept. You cannot alter what is certain. Don't find justification where there is no reason. Don't debate what is wrong. Accept your purpose and move on. You cannot live if you don't grow—and you cannot grow if you don't accept your failures. Your growth forms a stronger bond, but it is when you want to grow in your way that you find the walls are insurmountable. For your control is what holds you back. Grow to the stronger bond—and find the love, the trust, and the wisdom that bring acceptance and ultimately real purpose.

"To grow, we need the patience that our souls
deliver—and the relentlessness of our egos."

L ike a tree starts growing, it always grows with purpose and intent. The basis of its strength is found in its young years, where it sizes up the conditions, understands the wind, and nurtures a strong base to make its footing sure as the years progress. For this tree to grow healthy and strong, it needs patience because every season brings new lessons—and every season brings new conquests and needs more trust. For every season's lesson brings a rounded approach to everything in its path. Now as this tree grows in patience, in trust, it cannot grow strong only in one area and weak in others because it will not stand through the tests of every season. It cannot grow through the impatience of its fear or through a defensive attitude, trying to make it strong on one side but limiting growth in another. All seasons give lessons, every lesson gives strength, and all strengths contribute to character. That's why we need patience to grow strong.

May 30

*"The message of growth is often heard
in the sounds of silence."*

Nobody can say when we will hear or experience our lessons. It only comes through an acute awareness and understanding of our connectedness. It is therefore vitally important that we see, observe, and become aware of situations for growth that can be delivered through the wisdom of others. It is in these periods that we must allow ourselves the freedom to act from within, overcoming our egotistical fears and allowing that lesson and the growth associated with it to show its force. When our egos become quiet, we learn and grow. Be aware of the sounds of silence because that is when we grow.

"True growth happens when the ego loses control."

We think we grow through control. We think we grow when everything around us is in our immediate control. Nothing can go wrong, and our paths are plotted. True growth however happens when we show our hearts, and things change. Growth is the part of life that touches our souls, changes our opinions, and influences others through the lessons we learn. When we show our hearts, we reveal a plotted path that is true and not controlled through the egotistical means of fear and anxiety. Show your heart, and the world will change.

"Always grow but be patient with yourself."

As with all things, spiritual growth is a process. It is a process that starts with discovering and leads to your destiny. It is never in the habit of seeking perfection, as that is the ego's defense in being judgmental. It is important that, as we grow, we acknowledge our growth and find the patience to keep on striving for the next step, the next level, without looking back in a judgmental way, seeking perfection. As we become more patient with ourselves, we reflect that to others, and we become more patient with them as they grow and complete their processes. Growth is essential, but without patience, it causes egotistical frustration that stops the growth and changes our courses. We must always find the patience in ourselves and have patience so that everyone can grow in their own ways.

"Real growth requires as much thought as action."

We often think we are growing by thinking or that we are growing by doing. It is imperative that both happen. Our thoughts must be transferred into actions, and our actions must be transferred into thoughts. When this happens, we influence our programming, focus our thoughts, and reinforce them with the correct actions. And when we do the right things, our actions reinforce our thoughts—and that's how programming changes. It is the same with faith. So, we can't just think and grow or do and grow. We must think and do because then we truly grow.

June 3

"Let growth be your goal and water be your source."

I t is abundantly clear that life exists around clear water. Water is a life-giving force that creates beauty and shows the true nature of life. It is important for us to make our personal growth our goal every day. To grow toward our destinies, we need a water source, and it is important that we make that water source our souls. Let growth be our goal and let us grow from our souls. That will create life around us, show beauty in everything we touch, and give hope and courage to all those who connect with our water sources. Let growth be our goal and crystal-clear pure water be our source.

"Grow through the acceptance of your responsibility."

We often question the things happening in our lives. We often wonder about their meanings. It should be simple if we have the understanding of our souls to lead us through this process. Growth is about choices, and the fundamental truth in any decision is that we must accept the responsibility that accompanies it. Now when we grow on our paths, and our choices are clear from within, the acceptance of that responsibility becomes the pleasure that life brings to a well-lived life. Choices, growth, and responsibility are the three aspects that are key to a balanced existence in this world.

June 5

"Growth is not something we do. It is
something that has to be done."

Obstructing growth or finding ways to bypass it can never work. Following paths to avoid growth only leads to misery and pain. Confronting growth—not with a tantrum or egotistical approach but with a soulful understanding—leads us to learn and understand the message, the lesson, on our way. We can't grow by choice; we can't grow by force. We can only grow through acceptance. That is a surrender, and it is not an egotistical choosing; it's a soulful stillness. Growth will be there forever. For when we stop growing, we stop living.

June 6

"The more we grow, the less we remember."

Our journeys through life are filled with events that channel our paths and bring obstacles to our courses. These encounters leave us with memories that determine so much of what we do. The more we discover, the more we grow, the more these fade away. For we find that wisdom that erases those fears and allows us the freedom of tomorrow. So, the more we grow, the less we remember of that past that brings the anxiety that we always wanted to forget. So, to rid ourselves of fear is to discover that yesterday holds no power. For we live for today and the meaning of tomorrow.

The Obstacles:
The Art of Overcoming

People walk away from their paths
because they think they are difficult.
But mostly people walk away from their paths
because of their pasts.

It's overcoming evolution,
it's about overcoming engrained fears.
For the closer we get to understanding our ways,
the more we have to break the shackles of our pasts.

It's judging our paths through the eyes of yesterday
that makes it seem difficult.
It's letting go of the things
we feel are ingrained to our being.
And it's about understanding and accepting the things
that are ingrained to our souls.

People walk away from their paths
because they believe in their ego's importance.
People get to their paths
because they submit to their soul's determination.

"It's not about what happens to us—
it's about what happens within us."

We need to know that events around us can only affect us, either positively or negatively, but that it is all determined by how we handle things from within. When we see obstacles and not opportunities, we are forced to internalize the situations in different ways. We either push our souls to the side and listen to our egos or put our egos to the side and lead with our souls. When we are confronted with any problem, we always need to understand that we have the ability to conquer it, but we have to make the choice as to what center will drive our actions. Positive influence comes from our souls, and that is how we must always endeavor to solve what happens to us.

June 8

"The obstacle is what shows the way."

Blockages, barriers, and obstacles are there to guide and not to obstruct. They allow the ego to search for the soul's leading direction. They confront and ask for wisdom. They plead to look within and find help. This help is what is needed when we talk about programming. This help is what is needed when we talk about discovery. This help is what is needed when we talk about the ego's way or the soul's way and about identifying the difference. Make sure we are able to identify the obstacles because all of us are the help required to show the way.

June 9

"We only fail in the grips of sadness and despair.
The alternative is one of hope, trust, and growth."

The answer must be found in how we approach our obstacles and how we guide our thoughts and awareness. It is often found that when tears flow, our purposes grow. It's in the events, in the moments that we are called to stop and listen, that we discover our needs, our purposes, and our paths. We can only fail when we allow sadness, despair, and anxiety to infiltrate our lives and bind our trust in a ball of anxiety-ridden emotion that is kicked and passed from situation to situation. We have to protect against the frailty of the ego's notion of control because it is riddled with the complexities of fear and anxiety. We can only fail when we allow that to happen.

*"What do we trust more? The shield of
our souls or the walls of our ego?"*

The process of living is about risk and understanding. When we connect and understand our purposes, the shield of our souls will protect us through the values, the integrity, and the wisdom we know. When we are programmed with fear and anxiety, our egos build a wall that entraps our purposes and stops our growth. Walls are not to protect; they are to keep out or keep in. And so, as we evolve, we realize that less wall and more shield brings greater joy. Our souls understand the threats and will guide us through the values we keep. The ego will block us, and we will stagnate. Trust your soul's shield and wear it with purpose.

June 11

*"Obstacles are only there because
we want them to be there."*

In seeking direction, in following our paths, we are often doused in fear and anxiety because our egos, through programming and negative influence, try to stop our progress. The obstacles we encounter are only there because we fail to see the lesson, we fail to trust our growth, and we fail to hand over control to our purposes and the destinies designed for us. We must therefore not fall into petty influences in seeking control and fighting obstacles that allow our egos to find importance and detract from the purpose of the moment. Growth starts with understanding and then judging every situation to establish the correct course of action through insightful understanding of the reasons that exists.

"Dress yourself with a shield—
the shield of your purpose."

We have to accept that we will be battered or bruised during our lives. We will lack confidence, we will seek advice, and we will fall off our paths. It is our programming, our understanding, and our insight that can conquer all. It is therefore important to dress ourselves with a shield. Your purpose is your shield. It is the reason for you being here. It builds confidence, it overcomes obstacles, and it is the barrier that protects your soul from all the onslaughts of the world. We have to program our shields because they require a knowledge that we belong, that we are important, and that we have a real purpose to deliver.

"Obstacles seldom defeats us, faith in ourselves does."

When we believe, when we have faith, when we are connected with our souls, we understand our paths and our guidance comes from within. It removes the doubt—the insecurity that our egos try to force on us—because that is what makes us fail. Faith in ourselves means a clear path through our souls because we know our purposes. Understanding that the obstacles are mere learning curves on our road to a beautiful destiny will help us overcome them in a soulful way. Obstacles don't defeat us; they only grow us. Our souls will conquer all the obstacles we encounter—as long as we believe that our paths are the right ones. And that knowing can only come through being connected and seeing our purposes.

"See the challenges, embrace the opportunities because they are yours."

We must always remember that challenges and opportunities are on our paths to enrich us, to make us understand our paths better, and to help us overcome the obstacles of evolution and past wrong decisions. Challenges and obstacles may lead to frustration, but they are the biggest growth points we will encounter. The more challenges and opportunities we find, the more we develop and grow. It is when we stop—when we decide not to embrace the opportunity and walk away instead—that there is a sudden halt to our progress. Do not let the enormity of this world influence you. Do not let the size or difficulty of the challenge frustrate you. For your soul knows your capability. Your soul knows what you need to conquer the challenges. So, embrace your opportunities because they are there to guide you to your destiny.

June 15

"Vulnerability is to realize that you cannot be harmed."

When the soul shines through, we become vulnerable through our awareness. It shows the connection between our egos and our souls. It reveals that connection to the world, and it lets our egos accept the truth that they cannot be harmed. Vulnerability brings lessons that allow us growth, and it's important that the ego realize its importance because it must stand aside, and to do that, it must realize that it cannot be harmed. Vulnerability is the heart's biggest direction board, and it points us to what matters most. Allow your ego to realize that it will not be harmed.

June 16

"Always see the beauty in your obstacles."

All the obstacles we encounter—and all the bridges we have to cross—are there to lead us to purposeful lives. They either bring us back to our paths or give us opportunities for lessons required later in our lives. Obstacles are seldom seen as positive in our lives, but that should not detract us from the opportunities they present to grow us. We must see the beauty in our obstacles, find their purpose, and then accept them, deal with them in faith and trust, overcome them through understanding and wisdom, and find a clear way on the other side. The lessons they present reflect the care, the love, we have from God. We will only encounter the fear, the negativity, if we allow our egos to control us before we deal with the lessons they present.

"Don't search for happiness in problems."

Our lives dictate that we overcome the obstacles and solve the problems we encounter. This is a constant part of our daily existence. We must never focus all our resources on the problems or the obstacles and think we will find happiness when they are removed or solved. For this world will only give us the next problem—or an even bigger obstacle. Happiness exists because we are able to enjoy it. We are able to find it. It is not because we are different; it is only because we are constantly aware of our surroundings and our places in this world. Happiness comes from listening to our souls—and not through searching for obstacles in our egos or focusing on our fears and anxieties. Find the joy, and the problems will soon solve themselves.

June 18

"It is wonderful to suggest that every obstacle has purpose. It is true what they say that every cloud has a silver lining."

Every obstacle will find meaning; it is how we approach it that matters. Our souls seek positive light to grow and to find the paths we are destined for. It is our egos that fill us with negative feelings of anxiety and dread. We must then ask, "But how do I grow?" because growth through the ego can only be positive and sustained if it is driven through a quest that sits deep in our souls. We must govern our thoughts. We must remain vigilant. We must always strive to find love and a positive outlook on all we encounter. It is when we slump into the negative dread of fear that the obstacle becomes our meaning, and we forget about the meaning in the purposes we are here for. A holistic view generates positive light as our souls seek our destinies and our egos seek the moment. Positive light creates love, generates growth, and stimulates our attitudes about the future. Remain focused with the holistic view on your destiny because that generates the positive energy that feeds our souls.

June 19

"In clearing the path, we prepare for transition."

We are not asked to decide; we are not asked to make choices. All that is required is to guide toward the light. It calls for a forgetfulness that requires us to fulfill the last obstacles that are in the way of a clear transition. It requires of us to find happiness in despair. It requires of us to become less so that the soul can become more—and soar to the levels of tomorrow. In clearing the path, we will often find that the real event is placed in our way to make us reflect and make us understand that our real purposes are not about control, dominance, or self-importance in the situation, but they bring us back to understanding our own fallibility, our own limited understanding, and make us cherish the moments of today. For when we clear a path, we guide, not through the ego but through the soul.

June 20

"The darker the night, the brighter the star."

It is amazing how selective our memories are. We remember the pain, but we often forget the joy. We feel the scars, but we don't understand the healing. It is through the dark moments that we discover our brightest moments if we are aware and don't allow ourselves the selective memory that hides the stars behind clouds of anxiety and fear. The darker the night, the more we must look up to see the beauty in the sky. When we just focus on the ground, we lose our way. For these bright stars can be our compass, our inspiration, and our joy. It is in the darkness that we must trust that the light from above will always be present. We remove that certainty through unawareness and a wrong focus. We are given dark nights to discover our stars—so look up.

The Dream:
The Soul's Communication Tool

It's difficult to live one's life
without a view from the top.
For it's only at the mountaintops
that we can really see the world in all its beauty,
and distinguish it from the worldly glamour.

For on our paths, it's so easy to forget the beauty
beyond our everyday struggles.
So, we must live life with a view from the top.
Is it not true that climbing the mountain
can only bring reward in what we find
when we get to the top?

It's that view, that understanding,
that wisdom that we find
that fills us with hope and joy,
and makes the journey worthwhile.

We find that the more time we spend looking at the world,
the better we live in it.
For we allow our hearts to guide our minds
and bring order to this chaos.

So, this path that we have must never be viewed
from the eyes of our minds.

But it must be seen through the soaring wisdom of our hearts.
It's those comforts that bring us strength.
And it's that wisdom that gives us meaning.

So, to live this path, we must discover the ways
to view it from above.
For when we see tomorrow,
it makes today easier and brings meaning to yesterday.

Enrich our minds by allowing our hearts
to share a view from above.

June 21

"Life is only really lived in the reality of our dreams."

The beauty of our souls is truly the ability to project onto a vivid canvas all the benefits, the joy, and the happiness that can be found in living true to our purposes. It is important that we examine these dreams, these beautiful pictures and find the real ones that come from the soul—and not from the egotistical importance in this world. The reality that is hidden in our dreams is our link to living our purposes. The beauty of understanding them, of finding the wisdom, and revealing that to the world is our duty. We must always clearly find a way to allow these dreams to show themselves because that becomes the canvas of our lives.

June 22

"Harmony with the soul is found in the hidden pockets of imagination and dreams."

The ego's harmony with the soul—that connection, that bridge—gives us the balance to live in a joyful and truly meaningful way. It is the point we strive for. It's that harmony that makes us what we are. It develops us to be the best we can possibly be. It allows us to flow, and it allows us to find the hidden nuances that are so vital to our existence. That harmony is created through a willful and deliberate quest to understand our inner self. When we do that work, we discover the communication tools of the soul and of the ego. The main communication tool of the soul is through imagination and placing those dreams within the ego's grasp. Therefore, we must understand that if we imagine as a purpose, we must teach ourselves to discover the ones that come from the soul and from nowhere else.

*"Our true dreams reflect the sunshine
of the purpose of our souls'."*

The quest in life is walking the path and finding the purpose intended for our souls to reach maturity. The soul's purpose is changeable but exact. Through several means, we are able to achieve the same goal—and often we use our dreams to find our paths. The problem is in the identification of our true dreams. It is not in egotistical escapism; it is in the true merit that is our souls. It is important to spend time identifying our true dreams. They are hidden in the chapters of our lives, and they somehow form a constant line and have the ability to occur more than once. True dreams reflect the voices of our souls. They are the sunshine of our purposes. They burn away the clouds of rain and enlighten our way because they have meaning.

June 24

"Imagination has two eyes: one that sees the
positive and one that embraces the negative."

What we imagine comes from our souls or is forced on us by our egos. The ego brings us all the images that feed our anxiety, strengthen the fear, and withhold the growth. Our souls bring us the picture of trust, love, and possibility. Imagination is a privilege. When we apply it, it fills the voids and makes our paths clear and picturesque. With all the pictures we find coming from our souls, we embrace the growth, which leads us to our purposes. Imagination must be seen and experienced through the eyes of our souls.

June 25

*"Inspiration is the ego's enlightenment. Share
it and pass it on because the inspiration we find
is how our souls enlighten our heads."*

Pass it on. Share it. Inspiration and enlightenment guide our way. It is what we feel, what we live from inside, that brings purpose to others and fulfills our lives. Be inspired. For that will enlighten others to find their ways.

June 26

"Visualize your dreams—for therein lies your purpose."

nderstanding our paths is about understanding our futures. Visualizing our dreams will make them come to pass. It is in the visualization that our acceptance becomes clear. It is in the visualization that our guidance becomes clear. Seeing our dreams is committing to our futures. We can only accept the right dreams. We can only accept purposeful dreams. Therefore, our acceptance of our purpose lies in the visualization of our dreams.

"Let your dreams awaken you to your purpose."

Hidden behind the layers of egotistical defense in the shadows of our worldly expectations, hidden under all the fear and anxiety, are the dreams that can lead us to our purposes. Listening to the soft whisperings of our souls, we must identify the dreams that fit our paths because they can bring us to our purposes. It requires the absence of thought and the silence of ego to experience the real dream and make it real. Our own insufficiency must never stop us from exploring, but it requires that we do the work, that we work in the world, to bring our dreams to reality. That is how we grow in discovering our purposes.

The Navigation:
Following Guidance

The yearnings of your heart show you the path.
They want you to discover the meaning,
the value for your existence.

How we realize those yearnings
must be one of the lessons of our lives.

For we can realize them through our heads
and our egos will show us how difficult,
how filled with obstacles this life can be.

But when we surrender and ask the way ahead,
we discover that we open the doors
and we fill our lives with what is important.

When we are led by the spirit,
we encounter the beauty
and the wisdom of that path.

Unlike when we fight for control to show our own ability,
it's when we surrender and allow our minds to be led
that we are shown that what we need
is often more than we will ever know.

Let this journey come through the spirit,
come through the heart,
and not the reason of our heads.

*"Fear and anxiety are the product of our
thoughts, the product of our control."*

All beautiful things, all true miracles, are beyond control. They do not need human intervention. They require very little thought. Like the flower in nature, the creation of life, the end of life, are all beyond our control. Why do they create so much anxiety, fear, and complexity in our lives? The answer is found in the compass we use to guide us on our paths. The egotistical compass steers us to fear, anxiety, and control. It requires us to have full control and no trust. The soul's compass is fitted with purpose; it narrows our direction and guides us through trust and soulful purpose that points clearly to our destinies. The best gift in programming is a good compass. Let us think and hold the thoughts that come from the guiding compass of our souls because that becomes the trust we require.

June 29

"Search your soul's reserve for answers."

We so easily fall into finding answers in the world. We so easily change our paths for what we think we need. Our spiritual reserve, the wisdom of our souls, has an abundance of direction boards. We must search in stillness, tap into our reserves, and exploit the answers. They bring us wisdom beyond measure. Don't let the challenges of the world deplete the reserve of our souls.

June 30

"Plan with your soul—and your ego will follow."

It is imperative that we plan with our souls because when we plan with our souls, our plans are in line with our destinies. When we plan with the ego, we subscribe to anxiety and fear, and we force ourselves to plan away from trust, to plan for control. It is important that we plan, and when we plan to understand that certainty is not necessarily the outcome, but it is definitely in line with what our destinies require. It is important to understand that certainty is about knowing that the right plan will happen—and not necessarily the one we think should happen. Planning with our souls brings that certainty as we are planning on our paths, and that will force the ego to follow.

July 1

*"Our souls travel with a fixed destination
and a definite time of arrival."*

Not finding our paths, not knowing our route, is the ego's way of governing our lives. It means we travel with no fixed destination and no time of arrival. Our souls are born knowing our destinations. And as we travel, we fix our times of arrival. It is on these travels that we learn our lessons and understand our lives. For often when we go in search of meaning, our egos rob us of life. Connect with our souls—and we will find the fixed destination. And there will be no need to search for meaning because it was already given to us at birth.

"Find direction through obstacles in your mind."

Lessons and growth come in various forms. The obstacles our egos present, the barriers formed in our minds, are often the direction boards that lead us on our paths and fulfill our quests. Identifying these barriers and obstacles and seeing them for what they are can be the basis of finding direction on our paths. So, listen, learn, investigate, and evaluate the obstacles in your mind. They are as much your guide as understanding your destiny is.

July 3

"Navigating your life can never be done in a day."

Following our paths, navigating our ways, requires patience, insight, and the ability to listen. Trying to navigate all in one day ensures that we navigate through our preconceptions and guide ourselves with the fear of yesterday and the programming of the past. It is about the ability to use the lessons of the past; therefore, growth is progressive and is never a single event. It is important that we set goals, but it is more important not to seek perfection, fulfillment, in a single day. The slower the process, the more insight we get. And as this insight grows, the progress of growth speeds up. Don't navigate your life in one day. For that is often the path you don't need.

July 4

"The real answers don't come from our heads—
we must find them in our hearts."

What we think only brings awareness when we connect with our hearts. Searching for answers through intellectual debate only brings anxiety and reflects the impossibility of our dreams. The true answers come from our hearts because they show trust, reflect the possibility, and never seek the importance of others.

"Too much is as bad as too little."

We flood ourselves with everything. We require more and more. We search for more answers, and we need to ask more questions. And in doing so, we deprive ourselves of understanding. When we trust, we know that what we search for will be revealed. And that knowledge should be all we need to understand. We require the balance of soulful direction and egotistical ability to give us all we need to lead the way.

July 6

*"Every idea seems to be a good idea
until we find the right idea."*

Discovery and the process of learning must come from the exposure to difference. When we explore, when we seek different options, we learn and grow in wisdom, and we find the most fundamental fact of life, of our existence, namely our purposes, becomes clear. In this process of exploring, we find the wisdom that enables us to grow and teach others to find their purposes, their destiny. So, every idea can be explored, but we must remember that an idea should not lead to taking the wrong path because not every path is a good path. So, explore ideas because all ideas are good—until we find the right idea on our paths.

"Why not try to find the open door rather than trying to squeeze through the narrow hole?"

The ego always makes us walk the tightrope of approval. Our souls want to show us the open door and a wide, paved road to purpose. In this world, we don't find gratitude or show gratitude without the efforts that come from our souls. The ego forgets. It seeks short-term solutions. It wants to squeeze through the narrow hole to find that excitement. It holds us in an anxious space. For finding the open door requires trust, patience, and the efforts of our souls. Seek the open door—and not the narrow hole.

July 8

"Hope comes from our souls—and not from our environments."

Hope is the oxygen of life. It provides us with a vision for the future. It gives us reason to continue. Hope is the oxygen of our lives. Our souls provide the dreams, give the answers, and feed them through hope and love. Like hope, despair also comes from our souls and not our environments. Our paths are filled with hope, and when we are wrong, our paths are filled with despair. They both guide us to tomorrow, to our purposes, and to our destinies. Hope grows in love and feeds our bodies with the purpose we require to fulfill our destinies.

July 9

*"Awareness of every moment is essential
to live life to its fullest."*

Moments in time are not just anniversaries that we should celebrate; these moments in time must reflect the innermost path that will lead us to a destiny that is not often seen by ourselves—but often clearly understood by others. Destiny is a reflection of where our souls need to lead us, and these moments make us aware of the road ahead. It's important that we touch, feel, and acknowledge these small moments—whatever they may be—as direction boards to our destinies. So, we should teach, we should learn, about finding these direction boards and learning how to read them and follow them because that is what fills our lives.

July 10

*"Remember that life doesn't have to be
in a constant fight with you."*

When we find wisdom in our lives, things tend to be smoother, evener, and more in balance. It is this time that we know we are living from the soul through the ego and life becomes a pleasure— and not a constant fight. We have to understand that when life is in a constant fight with you, isn't it trying to tell you something? So, return to quietness, establish your connections, and find the wisdom that will smooth your way.

July 11

"You can never start a journey if
you are already traveling."

Perspective is the soul's way of showing wisdom. When we find the insight, we deliver the truths we require to continue. What we must remember is that we can't start if we haven't stopped. We can only change direction. We are often forced to stop, and at other times, we might just change direction, but on our journeys, we must always be alert and aware of what is required. If we travel too fast, if we lack the time to listen and discover the insight we require, we will continue to travel in the direction we are heading. It's only when we slow down that we can change direction. It's only when we stop that we can start again. Spiritual growth requires moments of stillness when we pause and consider the journey and when we stop, reflect, and search our souls to deliver the perspective we need to continue.

"A map takes you anywhere. A destination takes you somewhere."

When we enter this world, we soon learn that it is easy to find a map. It is a map with various paths that all lead somewhere. Over time, we learn, we grow, and we slowly define our purposes. And then one day, through all the lessons learned, we discover a destination. We quickly gather our maps and find the path that leads us to our destinations, which lead us somewhere. A journey with a map can be confusing if we don't know where we are going. A journey with the knowledge of our destinies brings wisdom and clarity to our maps.

*"Lead yourself to the open door because it can
take a lifetime to try open a closed door."*

Let our searches not only encounter the obstacles. Through the fear, we will always seek the barriers. During our searches, we must allow ourselves the freedom of the soul and the openness of the ego to explore and discover all the wisdom and answers that will lead us through all the open doors. Do not enclose ourselves to only find the barrier, the closed door, because that brings negative thoughts and the anxiety that stop possibility and take our searches back to the same places. Wisdom requires the freedom to create possibilities where the ego sees none.

July 14

"Do I choose the rocky road—or is it there for a reason?"

Our sense of direction for soulful purpose often leaves us in knots, and then we choose any road, any path, no matter what the obstacles we encounter. On our journeys, we must accept that not all will be plain sailing, because often it's the bumpy journeys that bring the most growth. It is these rocky roads that bring more direction and focus our purposes. So, yes, the rocky road has a reason. It is to shake my ego into accepting my soul. It is to cause insight in finding my purpose. It is to bring understanding to my journey that can lead to my destiny. When we choose the wrong road, we find no soulful bliss. We gain little understanding, except a knowledge, an awakening, that this is wrong. And through that reflection, we are guided to our paths. So, when we choose the rocky road, it also has a reason: to bring us back to where we belong.

July 15

*"Guidance is not about what we
know. It's about what we do."*

Positive thoughts, or soulful guidance, find no meaning unless they are converted into actions. Our purposes can never be just internal; they must be reflected through our actions in this world. The biggest obstacle is overcoming the fear in our minds, in the attitudes we display, and in the trust we portray. Action is the culmination of soulful guidance, and we must be aware that it is the balance we need between our egos and our souls.

"An open door is a sure sign."

A s we live and as we grow, we must constantly be aware not to ignore the open doors. For our progression, our growth, relies heavily on seeing the signs of our paths. Now an open door is a sure sign, but often our egos, the fear within, force us to close it, move beyond, and enter the area that we call *security of the abyss.* The ego's dominance will always lead us away from the open door. However, when we listen with our souls, we will see the open doors and trust their purpose. An open door is a sure sign. Enter in trust and confidence because locked in there is our purposes and the fulfillment of our destinies.

July 17

"The world will tell you what you want to know."

Our paths and our growth are filled with questions and answers. The answers are all around us. The world we live in will gladly give us direction. There is information at every point. There are many answers that lead us on many paths. The answers will never be the problem. It's the questions that are troublesome. The world will show you what you want to know, but it's what you want to know that should be the real question. When we live from within, we know what we want to know. And we find that direction from within. The world will show you what you want to know, but make it clear that you already know.

"Be aware of the stirrings in our spirits."

The stirrings of our spirits are not the voices of our souls or the calling of our egos, but the stirring in the spirit is our guide, calling, whispering softly, and asking us to listen. It points us directly to touch our souls. It surrounds us in protection, and it navigates us to our paths. The stirring in our spirits stops us and makes us see the wonders of the world. It blocks our egos from disappearing into the masses of popularity, pleasure, and an unfulfilled existence. The stirrings in our spirits are a guide. It knows our souls and brings us to our purposes.

The Timing:
Become Ready

Timing is never exact,
except to say that it is precise.

Timing is not a specific point,
but it is a specific point to another point.
It's where things interact; it's a position,
where two or more events coincide.

Timing is not exact, but it is precise.
For it needs the precision of all the events to coincide,
and that's not exact,
for it can happen at any given time.

As we grow, we learn to trust and wait in readiness
for, as things unfold, we grow.
But the more we learn,
the more ready we become to accept this goal.

You see, in timing, we must be able to trust
for that is the biggest element that gets us ready
to react when all the other events call on us to react.

Timing is everything when we are ready,
and nothing when we are not.

So, the more we grow, the more we learn,
the better we react when timing occurs.

July 19

*"Timing is not what is in our heads; it
is what is hidden in our hearts."*

Our souls know. They know the answers, and they understand our paths. Timing is not something in the ego's control; it is perfected through our souls' lessons. Timing does not bring control. It doesn't make our journeys easier. It does not understand our paths. Timing is nothing about the ego; it is all about the soul. The open door can only be seen when the soul is ready. Timing is about surrender and a lot about forgetfulness. The ego cannot wrestle and establish control through timing, but it must surrender for timing to occur.

July 20

"Timing is everything."

As life goes by, we must understand that there is a time for everything. Often what we really wanted, we already had, but we said no to. Often our destinies gave us all the opportunities, but we found ourselves unaware. Timing requires awareness, but it also needs acceptance that what we are given is right at the time, for that brings our purposes to their paths. Understanding spiritual growth, understanding the work, the effort, all relates to a simple awareness to accept and receive what we are given even though our egos may protest and fill us with the fear and anxiety, blocking that growth and understanding we need. That's timing.

"Trust allows our souls to have perfect timing."

When we are connected, when we lead through our souls, that empowers an effective life. When our souls are empowered through trust, it gives our lives perfect timing. It delivers the required elements for our purposes and our destinies at the right time, but timing is as much about trust as trust is about timing. Control is about where, when, and how. Trust and timing are about readiness, anytime, and peace. It is important that we stay connected to give our souls the freedom of perfect timing.

July 22

"To become ready requires time, but more so, timing."

We often live our lives as though we are waiting for time to pass. Readiness is not merely about time. It is not just about experience, about lessons learned, and about wisdom gained; it is also about finding and creating, observing, and accepting the perfect timing for our actions. Often waiting is better than acting. Silence is better than talking. For all of it requires distinct timing. The lessons are not learned through mere time, and they are often expressed better with correct timing. So, let's all understand the importance of timing. And let's reveal our souls' leadership through our actions and how we deal with the world in relation to the correct timing.

July 23

"Time is the great leveler in this world."

No matter what the peaks or the troughs, time levels everything. Time brings an understanding to our lives, to our pasts, and if we learn, to our futures. Time must be used in a way that grows us. Time spent on the wrong path, on issues and events that are harmful to us, our souls, and our purposes, is wasted. The more time we lose, the longer it takes to regain our composure and find the paths we are destined for. Time never forgets, but it brings a wisdom, a thoughtfulness, an understanding that grows those of us who use it to benefit our existence. Time has perspective and must be used in every moment of every day because that is what grows us. Let us grow knowing that the time we use must be the best we can use it for.

The Soul Path:
Walking with Your Soul

When you are walking with your soul,
you can hold your head high.
For you are walking with true purpose
with meaning truly defined.

For you know your blessings,
you live them every day.
Not because they boost your ego,
but only for they make this world a better place.

It's that humbleness that makes you aware
that walking with your soul
brings so much to bear.

It's the clear and open path that you follow
that makes every day a miracle.
It gives you strengths
beyond your belief.

For you are doing what is right,
and there is no shame or fear
or even a notion of defeat.

You will overcome
you will win in every way
if you walk with your soul
and find the truth in every way.

July 24

"See life through the window of your spiritual experience."

We spoil the beauty of the world through our egotistical arrogance and our narrow spiritual guidance. To really see the beauty, to understand it, we must see the world through the window of spiritual guidance. At first it is a small, narrow, and dirty window, but as we grow, as we accept, the window becomes bigger and clearer—and we view the world through the understanding of our souls. It breaks the ego's anxiety cycle. For when we view the world with a wide spiritual guidance, we find that trust replaces fear and light replaces darkness. We exist through the lenses of our souls.

July 25

"Let everything you do reflect everything you are."

It happens so often that what we are, meaning what our souls are, is not reflected through our actions. This is because we allow our egos to hide our souls' beauty in shame. To reflect what we are, what we really are, takes time, understanding, and an ultimate trust because it is not always the worldly thing to do. So, in reflecting our souls' quest to the world, we must stand proud in our beliefs, our trust, and our confidence in knowing we are on our paths.

July 26

"Our souls' constancy is our assurance."

When the connection between our heads and our hearts, our souls and our egos, is clear and strong, we find the true constant in this equation is the determination of our souls to lead us on our paths. It removes the barriers of fear, it allows us to see tomorrow, and it makes us warm in touching love and finding the purposes we are destined for. It overwhelms us with blessings, and it shows us that every moment is as precious as the one our egos seek. Our souls are constant, and they should be the trust center of our lives. Commit to your soul, and you will see the sunshine in your life, the joy in your existence, and the blessings of your being, illuminated in light.

"Happiness is hidden in our dependence."

When we know our purposes and we walk our paths, we find the value of our souls. The value steers us, it grows us, and it makes us dependent on the wisdom and the guiding force we have within. It is this dependence that brings clarity and happiness to our existence. It allows for less control and more acceptance. It is the knowing that the future will be bright—not by our standards but by those of our souls. In dependence, we find joy because that makes the impossible possible.

"The soul is equipped to handle every day."

Sometimes we forget that our paths, our purposes, come through determination and hard work because the lessons we learn are all needed to fulfill our purposes and to grow on our paths. We must remember that our souls have all the wisdom, all the answers, and all the questions we require to make the right decisions in fulfilling our purposes. The soul is equipped with knowledge, wisdom, trust, and the faith to guide us on our paths. The ego's obstacles, the short intervals of losing our way, are all little growth missions that ultimately, if we know our souls, when we make the connection, we will be refocused on our paths. Our souls have the equipment to fulfill our purposes—believe it every day.

July 29

"What's not made permanent by the soul remains a temporary illusion."

Our souls will guide us to everything permanent in our lives. When we attach ourselves to idealistic and temporary materials and egotistical objects, we seldom find the true understanding of permanence from our souls. Attachments must never be what we deem ourselves to be. They can never be what our souls require: mere objects that temporarily fill our lives to give us assistance to fulfill our purposes. So, we must see them as temporary, and we must seek the permanent objects of guidance from our souls.

*"Allow your soul to assign meaning
to things in your world."*

Our world is driven by everything our egos find meaningful. We are bombarded with everything that is perceived as valuable in the egotistical world around us. We require the ability to judge, and we often forget to live. Judging comes from doubt and insecurity, and living comes from love and understanding. When our souls give value to the things of meaning in our world, we soon discover a way of living that is filled with wisdom, beauty, and an understanding that assigns meaning to everything we require.

July 31

"When we know, we let go. So, how do we know?"

Knowledge brings comfort; comfort replaces control and ultimately fills us with peace. So, how do we know? How do we attain the knowledge required to allow us to let go of control? Spiritually, it is an easy concept, but it is difficult to attain because we find comfort and knowledge when the soul leads. When the ego goes in search of knowledge, it does so with control—and then we find very little comfort. It is important to allow our souls to lead the way because that is when we find the knowledge. This knowledge is a knowing that in our purposes, all events are mere moments that make us wiser for the future. The purpose-driven events are few, but they will clearly stand out. It is important to identify our egotistical control elements and turn them into soul-leading moments in finding knowledge, comfort, and wisdom.

August 1

"You don't need more; you just need better."

I t is the old debate of quantity versus quality. You don't need more faith when you have faith. You just need to change the quality of your faith. You don't need more trust. What you need is pure trust. Our souls will always strive to improve the quality of our lives. And to do that, there will always be a struggle between the ego's need for more and the soul's purpose of improvement. Make what we have better—and more will automatically be granted. For improvement in our immediate environment, be it spiritual or worldly, brings more to improve. Let's not always focus on collection. We need the time to understand and improve our gains.

August 2

"You are the creator of your own experience."

We attract energy in the same way we attract our destinies. We will always create experiences through the guidance and leadership of our souls. It is when we are off our paths, when we don't understand our purposes, that our minds fill us with fear. We attract the energy of fear and failure, moving away from our purposes and our destinies. A positive thought must come through a positive feeling. We are exposed to the environments we create. When we think disaster, we attract disaster. When we think purpose, fulfillment, and destiny, we attract joy and understanding. We create our experiences through the energy we attract, and we attract the energy through the guidance we find. We must make sure that that guidance comes from our souls—and not from our egos or a world that is filled with doubt and confusion.

August 3

"When your soul speaks, everyone will listen."

The soul will always mystify and put to shame the ego's performance. When we deliver from our hearts, the message is warm, it is clear, it is filled with forgetfulness, and it speaks of destiny. Through the simplest way, it has disguised and made abundantly clear in a method of communicating its message to everyone. When the soul speaks, the ego fades—and we must recognize the warmth, that telling feeling that we are now on our sacred territory and a path of distinction and destiny. When our egos speak, we fight fear and clash with anxiety. Our words and our mouths become weapons and preach no future and show no destiny. It's all about the here, the now, and the hurt inflicted. When our egos speak, we relate to the wrong programming, but when our souls form part of the communication, the warmth and the love guide and deliver the messages clearly. They reprogram and revitalize our quest to follow our paths and fulfill our destinies. We must always understand that our souls speak in warm and loving ways. Ways that make everyone understand the message is clearer, stronger, and full of meaning.

August 4

"It's through the processes in everyday life that we grow, that we learn, and that we establish our moments for future memories."

Now what is important about this is that we must remember that every day needs those processes. Each day needs our thoughts and actions, but we must find them through the light of our souls. We must never fear to embark on a process of work, of thought, and of searching. Provided that we do it in a submissive and forgetful state, first seeking guidance from within before showing the way. To be different can never be wrong because difference from the world is a strength that only a few can accomplish, but it must always be evaluated. Are we different from the world or just different from our souls? Richness is found in the poorest of things, but it does require an awareness that comes from the soul and not from the processes of the ego. Our connection is what brings the understanding of tomorrow, but in finding it, we must discover the processes of our souls.

August 5

"The power you have is not in what you display—it's in what you know."

Displays of power often bring no result. When our egos force control, we lose sight of our souls' wisdom. The power we have is in the knowledge we have gained. It is in the experience of our lessons. It is in the understanding of our purposes. For that power doesn't hurt; it leads, it mentors, and it shows the way. For it comes from the inside through a display of our outsides.

August 6

"The ego looks to the past for identity. The soul seeks the future for fulfillment."

Clinging to the past, to programming that ruins our paths, obstructs the delivery of our purposes. We stand in amazement when we find a well of energy and encounter our true purposes. Clinging to the past to form our identities removes our souls' ability to grow us to what we should be. It is when we lose, when we forget, the importance of ourselves and our pasts that the new us embraces the future. It is important that we allow the self to seek tomorrow because that is what drives our growth and allows us to discover our purposes.

"Change comes from one's soul. It is
delivered through our egos."

We must understand that a good tree cannot bear bad fruits. As our souls commit us to our paths to deliver our destinies, that change comes from within. As that change happens, it overcomes the obstacles and the barriers that our self-centered ways and egotistical importance have placed in the way. As this connection between our souls and our egos becomes stronger, that change is delivered to the world through our egos. When this acceptance of change is real—and the quest for our destinies is accepted by our egos—we are able to deliver joy and wisdom to others.

August 8

"Don't let the soul's tenderness be confused for weakness."

We often confuse the tender approach of the soul to a problem as the weakness that the ego wants to defend against. It is a weakness as perceived by the ego, but it is often the biggest strength of the soul. It is when we get into situations of conflict—of problem-solving and egotistical barriers—the soul's approach will be gentle and tender. It will stand back and listen. It will acquire all the information to solve and move forward. Yet the ego will perceive this as a weakness, and it will put up barriers to stop that tenderness from being revealed. Egotistical behavior will pounce on this tenderness, leaving deep scars for the ego to put up more walls and barriers. Defend the soul's tenderness, in love and kindness, and know where it comes from. We only need to look forward and understand its strength.

August 9

"It is easy to find inspiration in others, but
we must find inspiration in ourselves."

To inspire is a part of our purpose. To lend a helping hand, to lead the way, and to give guidance are parts of the soulful path. It is easy to look to others to find that inspiration, but when we find that inspiration in ourselves, we know we are fulfilling our souls' journey. We find that space where our wisdom shines, and the knowledge comes from a different source than our minds. We see how that influences the world and how it changes the path for others. It's then that we know our paths. Always remember that the journey is about inspiring our minds through the wisdom of our souls. For then we act in a way that benefits all.

"Growth is to make our vague reflection clearer."

As we walk through life, we reflect an image of who we are and of what we have become. Every day, we are allowed to become more. Through the experiences of the past, it is common that we allow our minds, our egos, to reflect that image. It reflects the fears, and it is a blurry and somewhat vague reflection. Through growth and understanding, we make that reflection clearer. We remove the ripple and a clearer vision of who we are slowly appears. That is the soul reflecting our value. We must understand the peace associated with that wisdom. Accepting it allows us to grow further, and our reflections become clearer.

August 11

"Let the awakening in your heart
become the change in your head."

When we discover and realize the joy and peace on offer, we explore our real paths. No matter how big the obstacles or how painful the change, we still are filled with trust and acceptance. The more we walk this journey of our hearts, the more we must change the fear in our heads. For it is through our minds that we bring doubt to what is true. The only way to build that trust is to do and explore more of the majesty that brings light to our days and fills our world with blessings. We must understand that the more we grow, the easier it becomes.

August 12

"Don't let the pace of the world take
away the beauty of your journey."

The pressure that our minds place on our existence is self-imposed. For that comes from the fear that our value is locked up in our achievements—and the idea of creating more through our own will and power. Our purpose is to find equilibrium where the pressure of the world can be balanced by our views of its beauty. This is not a state of relaxation, but it's a purposeful understanding that we live in trust, and that every day we fulfill to the best of our ability in the knowledge that we will be guided to where we belong. Our journeys are filled with so much wisdom and lined with so much beauty that we should never allow our own pressure to block us from seeing it.

August 13

"Tomorrow's fruits find their water and food today."

What we reap is what we sow, but it goes much further than that. For understanding our paths, our purpose is about giving our souls, our hearts, the stage. For if we feed ourselves with food from the world, we won't deliver the joy and peace from our hearts, but when we feed ourselves with the water from our hearts, we are destined to deliver the joy of our purpose. So, in whatever we do, we must continually ask: Is this the food from our hearts—or is it coming from the world? For what we put in today is not always immediately evident, but it will show tomorrow in our joy.

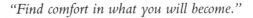

August 14

"Find comfort in what you will become."

The wisdom of our hearts, the guidance of our souls, will take us to peace and joy if we allow ourselves the freedom to follow that path. So, with all the obstacles and all the stresses and strains, be comforted by the knowledge that if you listen and follow the guidance, you will reach that place where understanding takes center stage.

August 15

"The reality is not what you live in the world—it is what you live in your heart."

The more we realize that our purposes, our destinies, are what bring the joy and abundance to our lives, the clearer we will understand where our realities exist. We must introduce that reality of the heart to the chaos in this world. For that acceptance of who we are brings light to this reality that we live in the world. It brightens up the space, and it helps the souls around us understand that the reality in our hearts means more than any other reality ever will.

August 16

"Freedom is something locked in our minds."

Our spirits, our souls, are filled with peace and know that tomorrow, the future, will bring the freedom to follow this path without fear or anxiety. We create the barriers in our minds, and we lock freedom away in sections of our minds. We overwhelm freedom with control, but we need to let it be. Awareness is not about passing time; it is about passing time with the understanding and the patience that allow our souls to exhibit that freedom and an existence filled with the determination of our purposes.

The Passage
of Purpose

The Path to Destiny

Live Your Purpose:
Your Value to the World

To unfold your hope
to breathe life into your dreams
means an acceptance of your destiny.

It requires that we trust our guidance
and that we believe in our paths.

It brings us to forgetfulness of ourselves
and a remembrance of the possibility
of who we really are.

As we grow, we learn that the difficulties
brought us the opportunities
to fill ourselves with wisdom
and to allow our hearts to keep us on track.

For the mistakes we have made will remain in the past,
but they are expunged
through the hope, the faith, the understanding, and the wisdom
that we know exist on our paths.

And when we follow that guidance,
we will grow in value to the world.
Not because of our own minds,
but because of the destinies of our souls.

*"Don't try to repair a tear to the heart
with a patch to the head."*

Our heads need debate and a reason to fix themselves. Our hearts require wisdom and understanding. We should never underestimate the purpose of the tears in our hearts. For with the head, we would like to fix it, to make it better, to debate it, but that's all ego and worldly. A tear to the heart brings forth wisdom and understanding. It's often not localized to yourself and brings a bigger picture, a greater message that must be shared, which will develop and release its purpose, to repair the tear and somehow help the world. Tears to the heart are fundamental to discovery. They are often the wounds of purpose, they reveal wisdom, and they connect to make us understand and fulfill the intended roles. Not every tear to the heart is a tear of purpose. For often what we think is a tear to the heart is just a blow to the head.

August 18

"We have each been given an acre of land, a portion of life. What do we cultivate on it? What do we grow?"

You see, in a well-lived life, we must look back and see the fruits of our labor, the beauty of our existence, and the results of our efforts. When we look back at our acre of land, is it filled with skeletons—or is it a beautiful garden filled with rosebushes? Is it a vineyard, bearing fruit? Is it a forest, giving life? Part of the process of being here is deciding what we cultivate. We are given free choice with only one parameter: it must fit within our purposes. So, when we get this gift, this portion of life, we must work at it. As a farmer grows the land, so we must grow our portions of life.

"There is no doubt in purpose."

When we have a purpose, and when we live with purpose, we have no doubt. The doubts we have are our own egotistical fears and anxieties conjured up through programming and experiences. It's through discovery that we remove these doubts and find faith in our abilities and belief in our purposes. Doubt cannot ruin the fire that burns through purpose. It must be discovered, and it must be addressed because it can be the biggest obstacle to fulfillment. Doubt is worldly. Purpose comes from our souls and is fed through wisdom. Do not succumb to doubt; instead, apply ourselves to purpose.

"Beyond what is possible."

Our spiritual dreams, our spiritual destinies, extend to what is beyond possible for our egos, our worldly understanding, to reach. The spiritual center forms the dreams and the basis that makes us centered in this world. It needs the connection, but more importantly, it needs our strength, our trust, to allow our character to stretch beyond what we believe is possible. That is when we discover the meaning of our purposes. It doesn't need to be the reckless disregard of the rules that govern our existence, but it does require that we seek the insight to explore the possibilities within the guidelines of our spiritual lives. When we ask the questions and knock on the doors of what our egos find impossible, we realize that our existence is not the reflection in the egotistical mirror of fear and anxiety. Instead, it stretches beyond belief.

*"It's the hard work in winter than
ensures a good harvest."*

Through the valleys and the hilltops of our lives, we must discover what is constant: the understanding that our souls' purpose leads us to become what we need to be when we listen. It's that wisdom that must comfort us through the hard times, through the winters of hard work, and will fill us with an understanding and the wisdom for tomorrow.

August 22

"Every day must be a destiny day."

The fulfillment of our purposes, reaching our destinies, is not a long-term or future event as much as it's about the fulfillment, the completion, of every day with that in mind. We must live goal-driven, purposeful lives that are filled with the wisdom and trust that whatever we busy ourselves with will bring growth to our purposes and energy to our lives. That is the completion of another step toward our destinies. We mustn't live for that one day in the future because we will miss all the moments of purpose—and we will lose the wisdom through awareness. Every day brings its growth. We can deny it, accept it, trust it, or abandon it.

August 23

"You can only love what you are doing when you discover the reason for doing it."

The guide to our paths must conquer many diversions, obstacles, and barriers to fulfillment. We can never understand it all while we live through the fear and negative thoughts associated with our egos. We will never discover the reason, the purpose, while we have the fear, anxiety, and negative commitments to our tasks. When we turn to trust, we lift the cloud and start to discover the reason. That is how we find the love we need to bring purpose to our daily tasks. The fear and the anxiety will never allow us to discover the reason, the purpose, because of all the lessons and barriers on our paths. When we reach the highs, the connectedness, we can look back and understand the growth, the love, and the joy in the fulfillment of that task. If you search for the reason, you will soon discover your purpose.

"To fly, you must first jump."

Life's privileges can only be owned by taking the risk and breaking free from the fears and anxieties of our egos. To soar on wings requires the courage to jump off the cliff in trust, faith, and a knowing that is reflected through our souls' wisdom. It is when we are burdened with fear that we prevent our souls from accomplishing the goals, the purpose, of our destinies. Reckless is also not the answer, but willful introspection will always allow our souls to get us ready to jump. The message to all must always be that lessons are in preparation to get us focused and ready to take flight. We must teach not how to fly because the soul already knows how, but we must teach when to jump.

August 25

"The purpose of today is to show your understanding."

Every day, we are confronted with different forces, and all that is required is that we allow our wisdom, our understanding, to shine through. When our purposes are linked to the way we live every day, we soon find peacefulness. Everything in this world requires soulful perspective and a heartfelt understanding. We don't spill over with ego—and we stand our ground—because we understand the lessons. Not just for ourselves—but for everyone we are touching. In our purposes, we must be understanding, and we will find that happiness comes from the wisdom we deliver.

"Accepting our purposes requires action."

t doesn't help that we walk our paths, that we follow this route that leads us to wisdom, but we do nothing. Accepting our purposes requires action. It requires that we do, and it requires that we actively engage in working for the fulfillment of our destinies. Thinking about it, reasoning, and debating it cannot be seen as action. Engaging with others in the acceptance of our purposes is what's required. A purpose is often a lonely affair, but it must be understood that our souls' journey will always require us touching other souls. It needs us to teach, it requires us to learn, and it requires us to do. When our purposes become ideals because of philosophical debates, they have little meaning.

"Finding the promise you made to yourself means
you have to work through many wishes."

A life's journey starts with countless wishes. It will entertain many diversions, opportunities, and disappointments. To understand this journey, we must enjoy all its fruits and fight through all its obstacles. The sooner we uncover the promise we have made, the quicker we will gain the peace and tranquility that this journey can offer. We must understand that every wish, every opportunity, every barrier, and every obstacle can lead us to our promise. It is therefore important to find the awareness that brings us closer to our purposes.

August 28

"The lessons we learn should be the lessons we teach."

Our lives—and our journeys—are not about a single event, purpose, or destination. They are filled with numerous lessons and with many small purposes, but holistically, they combine into our purposes. The lessons we learn, the obstacles we overcome, must be the experiences we use to make this world a better place. Our purposes, our destinies, will always follow in the experiences and lessons we have learned. So, when we grow, our biggest and only true meaning must be to show others the way.

August 29

"Let your vision construct your every day."

The detail is very important, but it is often destructive when we become so involved in survival that our paths, our visions, our purposes, are distant things and only important tomorrow. We must make every day part of our visions, our paths, and our purposes. With slow steps and long sweeps of the brush, a painting becomes a picture. We must discover that every day is essentially part of our tomorrow, and we must construct it in a way that helps fulfill our visions, our purposes. So, don't get lost in the detail, and always remember that every color can only be beautiful when seen in the completed picture.

August 30

"Find purpose in simplicity."

It's our nature to overcomplicate. We believe that the more we analyze, the cleverer we get. Find strength in simplicity. For the straight and narrow is often the right way to go. When we overcomplicate and overanalyze, we search for the anxiety, the fear, that would stop us from achieving our purposes. Clarity reveals itself through faith, trust, and experience—not through searching—because we believe it quells anxiety. We seek to learn, and we must understand that we already know.

August 31

"Purpose is found in the questions we ask."

It doesn't help doing nothing. Apathy leads to more anxiety. That is the ego's way. The ego will either divert and make us do what we shouldn't or stop us from doing anything. Purpose is found in the questions we ask. The answers are there. To search, to keep on knocking on the different doors, will soon show the ones that are closed and should remain closed and those that are open to grow us. Finding our purposes is work. It is often hard work, but we need to learn the lessons and gain the experience. Isn't that part of our purposes? To ask questions well also entails that we listen well to ourselves and to others. Don't allow your ego to block what you should hear. For that makes asking the questions also of no value.

"Attempt great things."

The soul's purpose is to find the reason that makes us unique and displays our purposes to the world. It requires that we grow through lessons, that we understand our evolution, that we seek our destinies, but above all, that we teach and leave the world better and wiser than before. The soul wants to attempt great things, but our egos block us through fear, anxiety, and control. The great things that our souls want us to achieve are clear and marked with big signposts on our paths. Our egos somehow fill our paths with mist and darkness, and the only way we clear this is to step in through faith and belief that our paths will clear and guide us to our destinies. The stronger our faith becomes, the more the mist lifts and darkness turns to light, and the clearer we see, but if we don't attempt great things, we will never find that clarity.

September 2

"Deliver your beauty without your ego seeking reward."

When we think of contributing to the world, we often think of it in an egotistical and self-rewarding manner. The beauty about the soul delivering its message to the world is that it seeks no reward. It does not look for acknowledgement, and it does not need approval. All it needs is a space to deliver its message. The ego sometimes delivers messages of compassion and love to this world, and it is much needed, but in return, it needs reward, acknowledgement, and approval. When this happens, we need to strengthen the focus of the connection between the head and the heart. The obstacles will soon be removed because when your ego delivers, it will encounter barriers, but when your soul delivers, it will be on your path. All that is needed is the work required to fulfill your destiny.

September 3

"Grow into your purpose."

We must accept that our reason for being must have a purpose. All our lessons, all our experiences, all our fears, and all our obstacles are lessons to make us more and more fulfilling and growing into this purpose. It is important that we start searching for this purpose, this reason for being, as early as possible. The sooner we come to terms with it, the better equipped we are to lead others through growth on a fulfilled path to their destinies. We must clearly evaluate all our lessons in accordance with insight, awareness, and knowledge to clearly define our purposes.

September 4

"We have many tasks but only one purpose."

During our lives, we will find ourselves chasing many quests and fulfilling multiple tasks. Some of them will be egotistical conquests that have very little meaning, but other soulful projects will give us the lessons needed for growth. All these tasks and projects push us and grow us in the direction of our destinies in the discovery of our purposes. And as wisdom fills us, we complete all the tasks and all the projects and will be left with our purposes. Understanding our blessings makes fulfilling more tasks easier because it is all part of our purposes.

September 5

"To deliver your purpose, you must do your part."

Do not think that the time in this world will be spent in the hands of the universe. The time in this world requires our active participation. It requires that we invest our time and effort into the right path. It requires that we discover, that we learn, and that we elaborate on the lessons to create understanding. It requires that we take the wisdom we receive and add our value to make it important to the world and to tomorrow. We must play our parts, and understanding our parts requires thought and connection.

"Shh, be quiet, be still because then
your destiny will find you."

Destiny, one's purpose, is often like a beautiful butterfly. When we chase it, it will escape, but when we sit still, when we are quiet, it will find us. Our destinies, our purposes, are not what we chase. It is the small, but important dreams that we know exist, that we find within our power, but have never been important enough to actualize. We chase the world and often mistake that as our purposes, as our destinies, but we must learn that in quiet contemplation, we will understand the dreams that are real and linked to our purposes. Shh. Be quiet.

"It is often our needs that suppress our purposes."

What we need, what we think we need, and what we really need are vastly different when we view them with an objective vision from our souls. It is important that we understand that the needs of this world must be balanced against our souls' need to learn, to grow, and to fulfill their purposes. It's through fear and anxiety that the ego disturbs this balance, and it's important that the discovery process unravels the complexity of our needs. What we need is really the fulfillment of our destinies. Never let that be obstructed through the visions of our worldly needs.

September 8

"Become the workhorse for your soul, and in time, your destiny will be delivered."

Become the workhorse for your soul, and your answers will be revealed. This means that you must submit the ego and forget that arrogance about wanting everything now—or knowing everything now—and do the work that your soul requires you to do, whatever that might be. In the time that you become the workhouse and allow for that work, your destiny will be revealed.

*"Let your soul be the candle that
delivers light as you grow."*

To deliver light on our paths is every soul's universal purpose. If the soul is the candle, then awareness is the wax, knowledge is the wick, and insight is the flame. Our souls must burn this candle to bring light and to attract others from their darkness, to light their flames, and to bring more light. Let our souls light the way because that is a big part of our purposes.

Service through Leadership:
Help Others Find Their Way

All of us must walk our chosen paths.
We chose them and designed our lives around them.
Often, we question the chosen path,
but what we must trust is that our souls will guide us
to bring purpose to our lives.

It calls us to awareness, it makes us work a lot,
to search for answers and discover the lessons.
We must learn to bring meaning to others.

For all that chosen path is, it is the way to elevate ourselves
through service and growth
to become more than just human,
to deliver better service to this world,
and to unite in love everything we find.

So, evaluate our chosen paths
and make sure they follow our hearts.
For when we lose our way,
our hearts become silent—and our minds become loud.

So, through the growth, we must find the solutions
to discovering the ways
to help others find their chosen paths.

"True leaders follow well."

To stand up in conviction, to understand your soul's answers, means you have to follow your purpose, and that will bring meaning. To become the leader, you have to become the follower, often not the follower of the world, but the follower of your heart. Leadership requires strength, and strength is found in the crevices of our souls. And to reveal it, we must discover our own unique purpose and follow it to leadership.

September 11

"Let your soul become the mirror to others."

Reflecting your growth is an essential part of achieving growth. That means that we must never allow our growth to be hidden behind the high walls of our egotistical fears. Reflecting our growth shows others who need assistance and development the way forward. It is important that we allow our souls to become mirrors, allowing others to look into the mirrors and see their futures. Mirrors reflect in silence, and they are not judgmental, forceful, or partisan. They allow others to find their own ways through the reflection of our souls. If our lives become the guiding mirrors, our souls will fulfill the essential part and purpose of helping others.

"Positive influence is what changes the world."

Programming and influence are so important to our lives, to our futures, and to the benefit of all. When we influence someone, we don't just influence or program the individual—we influence and program everyone they touch. Our reach becomes an ever-increasing circle, and when we are blessed with wisdom, knowledge, and leadership, our influence starts changing the world. Programming and influence are what change people's lives and connects them to their purposes, their souls' destinies. Positive influence grows our souls, enlarges others, and makes them reach their potential. The light of influence can lead anyone to his or her soul.

September 13

*"Insight is all about understanding
others through our souls."*

Understanding the world requires the insight, the wisdom, of our souls. When we find this wisdom, as we discover insight, we shouldn't lock it away. We must share it. Understanding the complexities of this world brings clarity and leads us in showing others the way. Wisdom must be shared, and we must show through our own behaviors that we understand and have the insight, the wisdom, to deal with others. Each soul will reach out to touch the wisdom and find the insight. If it is only ego, fear will stop the soul from moving toward that insight, that wisdom. Insight is not about us; it is about understanding wisdom and how we show it to others.

September 14

"The soul doesn't rescue—it educates."

Our egos need the importance, our egos need the acknowledgment, and our egos rescue because that brings it favor. It is the soul that educates. It wants to show others the way—not lead them or overpower them—to follow our way. It is the soul that frees others, and it is the ego that keeps them captive. Let's remind ourselves when we want to help. Are we doing it with our ego or are we educating through our souls?

September 15

"Let your soul be your limit."

We must never limit ourselves—our thinking, our boundaries, or our possibilities—by the influence of others. True leaders limit themselves from within. Their possibilities are guided through wisdom and the understanding that trust can make anything possible. They stand their ground because they know that tomorrow is what they see—and not what others show them or tell them to see. Their soul can express itself because it leads through faith and trust. We mustn't give in to the influences of the world because that limits our thinking and empowers our egos. Let our souls set our limits.

September 16

"Open souls will always recognize each other."

On our journeys, we must learn to identify the signs of a closed or open soul. Open souls recognize each other. They find no barriers and communicate what is dear and important to their purposes. To teach, we must be able to identify the closed soul. It is blocked and will exhibit different actions to show, to identify, its barriers. It allows the ego to retract and not participate in other places. It will force the ego to dominate. It often uses debate and reasoning to prove how open the soul is. That should always be a clear indicator of how blocked it is. To teach well, we must sense the energy and identify the obstacle that shows us how the heart is being obstructed. By identifying if a soul is open or closed, we gain the knowledge and the wisdom to help it build a bridge to its first connection.

September 17

"Be in tune with the silent cries—and not always with the loud shouting."

Our souls will always guide us to hear the need, to understand the help, to plot the path, and to guide to fulfilling a purpose. The ego makes us respond to loud shouting and to those who make it known that they are crying for help. The ego is protesting fear to hide the soul's agony. We often ignore the silent cries from a soul in need of wisdom. Our awareness should never be just egotistical, and we must find the strength of feeling to listen in silence. Hearing the cry and responding to it gives soulful meaning.

"Let your voice sprinkle light."

So often, our voices sow darkness. It hurts, and it causes scars because it comes forth from our egos. Its source is our baseless fears and anxieties. It is important that we make our voices the greatest source of joy and light, to uplift, to show beauty, and to guide us to the still waters of tranquility and peace. When this happens, our source is the soul because it is so easy to use this great tool to harm, to judge, and to express what our egos need to defend. So, we must use our voices to sprinkle light, and in return, our souls will enlighten us.

September 19

*"This is the time to teach through the
soundless word of your soul."*

Giving back, showing, and leading from within gives others the meaning they search for. It is the meaning that doesn't come through egotistical talk, but it is the meaning that is shown through love and strong connections. It is the soundless word that defines who we are, and in this time, we must teach and show others how to see with the eyes of the soul. Blindness of the ego lights up the star that guides us and guides us on the path to purpose.

"Our importance is found through
integration and not isolation."

We must understand that we live in this world, that we have a purpose in this world, and that we must integrate with this world. When we isolate ourselves, we lose the importance we need to fulfill our purposes. We cannot be sidelined though egotistical fear and anxiety and become commentators on the world we should be a part of. We are required to integrate ourselves and teach. Teaching never happens in isolation. For when we do it all ourselves, we transfer no knowledge, develop no skills, and have no importance except to say, "We have been here." We must deliver the wisdom and the knowledge though integration, delegation, and working with and becoming a mentor—and not merely a worker.

September 21

"Always ask, 'Is my will the best
way for my soul to lead?'"

Leadership is not a quality that can be taught to the ego; therefore, to be a good leader, lead from within. Firstly, lead yourself, and then your soul will shine through to lead others. So much of the ego's sense of control is to enforce our will and let our dominance shine through. The funny thing about the will is that it is what other egos respond to in the short term, but true leaders, successful ones, do not let their egos' sense of control make their souls submissive. They allow their souls to become the senior partners and lead the process. Leadership is not about dominance, fear, anxiety, or control.

"Leadership starts with a knowing that you belong there."

You cannot lead if you don't believe that you are in the right place. You cannot change, you can't affect growth, if you do not believe that you are the one to make those changes and take that leadership position. That requires a self-belief, ownership, vision, and the understanding and knowledge that this is your destined path. All you can do is trust, believe, and lead from the knowledge that you are in the right place.

September 23

"Collecting means nothing. Sharing means everything."

n collecting wisdom, we only feed our trees. However, when we bear the fruits, we must share them. The more we collect, the wiser we become about understanding the need. It is important that this process teaches us to listen well. That is how we will find the direction to go. Collecting must be about sharing.

September 24

"To enlighten others is to enlighten yourself."

Hope is not reserved to conquer the fear of our minds, but it is often the guiding cry from our souls that wants to lead us in discovering enlightenment. By giving others hope, we allow our souls the opportunity to connect with our minds. For in the guidance of others, our souls also guide us. It is important that we live through understanding that hope creates, gives expression to dreams, and builds. When there is an absence of hope, fear and anxiety prevail. So, enlighten others, but also enlighten yourself, by bringing presence to a future and giving guidance through understanding that wisdom is generated through the smallest discovery. That discovery in others—and in ourselves—gives us hope, unlocks our dreams, guides us, renews the old, and focuses the new.

September 25

"When we follow, we show true leadership."

True leadership is as unique to our souls as understanding our destinies is to our egos. It requires that the ego follow the soul in exhibiting leadership. We need to follow and become quiet to allow our souls to show us the way. We need to become forgetful to determine the right choices. We need to show that strength is in following a path—and not in displaying power. Leadership is unique to the soul and the ego because it can prove balance, or the lack thereof, when used in the wrong ways. Leadership is about leading our own lives and leading those around us. Become the follower, and you will soon be the leader.

"Become a soundboard for souls."

A soundboard amplifies sound. It allows sound to bounce off it, strengthening it and making it louder, or absorbing it and making it softer. We must become like a soundboard to listen and amplify the soul's message. Be it our own or others, we must listen and amplify the right message. We must become the soundboards for the good path. For when we are the soundboards for this egotistical world, we become loud with no direction. We scream for the wrong and allow the soul's sound no entry. Becoming a soundboard for the soul requires an understanding that we are the pillars anchored on rock, immovable, yet we are filled with compassion because we accept the sounds and amplify what is right. Become a soundboard and attract all the souls because they need a voice—and they need direction. The amplified sound shows clear direction.

The Tools of Wisdom

Prerequisites of Path

Awareness

Every moment needs awareness
for it's in that moment that wisdom can flow
or our heads can dominate.

Every moment requires awareness
for it's when our heads need control,
it's then that we let go of the awareness
and grasp the power of control.

Patience and awareness are the beautiful tools of wisdom.
They know when to talk, and they know when to keep quiet.
They understand when to control
and believe that through trust we gain so much more.

So, use these tools and use them well.
For wisdom grows our joy,
for we understand the moments
and we live through our hearts.

September 27

*"Awareness means keeping all the
channels of communication open."*

We have several connections that are important for our ultimate paths and purposes. The first, is between our heads and our hearts. The next is between our heads and our hearts and the world. And ultimately, those three are connect to God. All these connections require channels of communication. They require an awareness, an understanding, of how, when, and what is communicated. Now our single-minded approach is often limiting to our awareness because it seeks to listen, to feel, to touch, and to see, but those are only the obvious communication channels. Awareness is also about trust, when to surrender, emptiness, and fullness. They are feelings, emotive communication expressions, that help our souls guide our egos through energy sourced directly from our purposes. So, we must teach, we must show, that awareness is about a lot more than the obvious channels of communication.

"Every day is an awakening."

L ike the sun rises, bringing life to the new day, so every day, every moment must be an awakening for us. An awakening in gratitude, an awakening in wisdom, an awakening in walking our paths, in fulfilling our purposes. As the sun brings life to the day, so these awakenings bring life to our existence. We must always awaken with the positive flow of energy from above, pulsing through our bodies, because we know. In a life driven by purpose, our awakenings keep us focused on our paths and our purposes. Let every day remind us to awaken, and we will.

"It's when we treasure the moment that we find direction, and it's when we find the direction, it is then that we understand what awareness is about."

Awareness is a constant series of lessons. The more aware we become, the better we learn. It is through these lessons that we understand tomorrow. Awareness must be about exercise. It must be about devoting time to creating awareness because it is in the moment that we find direction. Awareness must be forgetful for a basic principle to great awareness is not to judge; it is to absorb. And when we absorb, we reflect the light that is our purpose. Growth, discovery, and purpose are all influenced by awareness. We find direction in the moment. Make sure we are always aware of the moment.

September 30

"See every moment as you should."

It is amazing how we let the good pass us by and allow the bad to keep our attention. It is amazing how aware we are of our problems but how forgetful we are of our blessings. We remember everything we don't like, but we fail to see the benefits and the things we do like. Our lives must be balanced. Putting too much weight and awareness on difficulty lets our egos triumphantly celebrate anxiety and fear. We avoid situations for the fear of not knowing and not being aware of the good that might come from them. We think that staying away and focusing on the security of what we have brings more peace and less trouble. How wrong we can be. Awareness is about growth and not avoiding. Awareness is about understanding. We should focus on every situation.

October 1

"The greatest gift to yourself is awareness."

The ability to understand and follow our paths comes from our souls' ability to have the wisdom. It comes from trust, and it grows through awareness. The greatest gift to the soul is the forgetfulness that the ego brings through awareness. It sees the opportunity in our paths and allows our souls to make the correct choices. It determines our futures, not through fear, but through inner trust. Give yourself awareness every day because that shows the wisdom in your connection.

October 2

"It is awareness that filters our oil to burn our lives."

As we grow and develop in this world, we get oil—life-sustaining fuel—to burn the light that we call our lives. This light illuminates and shows us the way. It can be burning dirty oil, flickering low, or raging out of control. Or we can filter it through the awareness of our souls. This filter becomes the step into our futures. What goes through it ensures that our paths will have a steady light and will open up the lives of countless others. We must always remember our pasts; that is one component of the filter, but awareness often requires more that we remember our futures. Don't think about the future or forget the future. Instead, create the memories that were planted in our dreams about the future. Awareness filters like our hearts connect to the world, and we must always constantly be aware of its power.

October 3

"Today's answers should always be tomorrow's questions."

When a path is followed that leads to destiny, the answers you get today will always be so apparent that it makes your way clear, free of fear and anxiety, and in total confidence and trust. It is when we forget these answers that we relinquish control of our souls' biggest asset, awareness, and that is why we must always guard these answers. Answers define the way ahead, and tomorrow's questions should sprout like a tree, all from the same answer, and deliver the options that are clear for the future. Our souls' answers, our quests for our destinies, all come from within. The answers will always be there; it is merely about finding the correct questions. Always find your answer, live by it, and make tomorrow's questions relevant to them.

October 4

"Awareness brings abundance to our lives."

As we go through life, we need food and water to stay alive. Awareness is the spiritual food that makes our lives abundantly full. It becomes our bread, and we nourish ourselves in understanding and wisdom. Make sure we feed ourselves with awareness every day.

October 5

"An awakening is when dreams and reality meet."

We can have several awakenings in our lives. It is the awareness, the understanding, that makes an awakening real or just another moment of egotistical irritation. When our souls meet our minds in a purposeful place, it brings meaning and understanding to our lives. It is this awareness that we need so much of. It allows an awakening to bring purpose to our paths. Awakenings bring meaning, but they require our intent and must be recognized as the first connection that leads us to deeper meaning and growth. Misfortune or joy—there are too many to name—can all be there to awaken us to the real meaning and to introduce the real you to yourself. Be aware.

October 6

"Awareness makes us see a rainbow through our tears."

Awareness must be the ego's guide. It is the soul's way of leading. When we stay connected, we will find that the joy from our souls, the peace and the understanding are always present. Through all the happiness, sadness, milestones, and growth we achieve, our souls' joy is always present. It is important to understand that the awareness we find in our everyday lives should not be fleeting, and we should nurture it. It is the guide that we can rely on to lead us. Seek the joy and find happiness wherever you go. You will find your purpose through that awareness.

October 7

"Let your soul be alert—and not your ego."

Awareness must come from within. The ego's awareness seeks the negative, the fear, and the problems. The soul's awareness touches all we need to find all we are.

October 8

"Growth is actionable awareness."

The twin of awareness is growth; one can't exist without the other. For us to grow effectively, we must establish and nurture an awareness that is founded firstly in our discovery process. It is important to understand that through awareness, seeds are planted, and they need water for growth. Awareness allows us to identify these seeds, nurture them, and water them to achieve growth. Awareness becomes the actions we require to make growth happen.

October 9

"It is the bright lights that awakens us—
and never the pit of darkness."

Over time, we are programmed to love living in darkness. We touch around and feel our way because we find comfort in the problems and the obstacles our egos create. It is the negativity that feeds. Awakening comes through positive awareness. It changes the mind and focuses on what is possible. It controls the ego and conquers the fear. It is that light that grows us. There is no better plan than a plan because the alternative is nothing.

October 10

*"It is your awareness that makes
love complete and perfect."*

Awareness is the food of love. It feeds it, and it makes us understand how fantastic and complete and joyful it is. It shows us the depth of God. Awareness is the source, the beginning, of a life lived, of abundance and joy through love. When we are aware, we see, we feel, and we understand life's true beauty. It is not because of what happens outside; it is because of what happens inside us. Awareness is what love needs to create the path that gives us purpose to the end.

Trust

When a journey feels littered with trouble,
when our paths feel too steep to climb,
it's of no use to become angry and frustrated,
for it only brings more problems to the steep climb.

It's then that we need the understanding
that our souls can provide.
For it's not in solving the problems
or trying to understand why,
but it's in finding that peace and trust
and letting go of our own control.

For the more we struggle, the harder it gets,
but the more we trust, the bigger the grace we receive.
For when we trust no mistakes can be made,
we must do the work and trust that the ending is in sight.

We cannot be frustrated because trust reveals the promise
of knowledge beyond our comprehension,
beyond what we think possible.
And it will fill us with the joy
that transcends our own ability
to try to find happiness through our own means.

So, when the path is steep and the journey feels troubled,
trust more, love more,
and soon you will find a calmness that clears the path
and brings us the right light, the right decisions,
and makes the journey the correct one.

October 11

"Trust reflects your soul's wisdom."

When we walk this journey, we learn and experience everything we require to become successful in our purposes. When we trust that journey, we find that we act in accordance with our paths, and we listen to the wisdom of our souls. The ego will always try to limit that trust because it is not a reflection of the ego. Trust reveals the knowledge we need to successfully grow and evolve to fulfill our destinies.

October 12

"To really trust, you must have control."

To understand trust is to understand control. Control of our environments and our lives doesn't always originate in our heads—or through our egos. To really trust is to find that control in our souls. Not all choices should be made in our heads because that confuses and awakens fear. To find that trust is to allow our knowledge to control our heads and our egos. To remove fear through trust is to allow our souls to control our lives. This is the balance, the connection, between our souls and our egos. The control we know that stems from our heads stands back and makes space for the control, the trust, that comes from our hearts.

"Trust is what makes the impossible possible."

Control and an egotistical life wrestle trust away and turn it into anxiety. It's the constant fight to prove to ourselves that we know best. That we will carve our destinies the way we think it should be. Trust's biggest ally is not apathy; it is an absolute dedication to do all that is required and in doing it, accepting the outcome through the lessons and wisdom we gain. Control takes our thoughts and makes the possible impossible. It prevents us from realizing that tomorrow is about the wisdom we find today. It is not about the fear we show to all who grow with us. To exhibit trust is not to be neglectful of finding answers and growing in this world; it is everything about acceptance, and it often leads us to a forgetfulness that brings peace and joy to our journeys.

October 14

"Trust brings confidence."

The soul needs a confident ego, an ego that is not trapped by fear, that trusts its purpose, and that seeks its destiny. Confidence breeds adventure because it is free of anxiety, and it searches for growth. It grows on its path through obstacles and finds the understanding because it trusts. Confidence never comes first. We must trust that it "will be" to enable the ego to find the confidence to "let it be."

October 15

"The trusted road brings a peaceful journey."

Our lives, our choices, need to be filled with the soulful promise of peace. This tranquility makes us walk the road with confidence and an understanding of our purposes. It is important that we take the trusted road because that is the soul's choice. It requires that we listen, plan the route, see the map, and choose the road of peace and wisdom. It is not always the biggest or widest road, but it is the one that fills us with a quiet confidence and the knowledge of our purposes, our role, in this journey.

October 16

"Trust is never evident in control."

In life, the fine balance between trust and control makes our souls light up our paths. It is striking the balance where the connection between our heads and our hearts determines the way. It is understanding that where there is trust, there needs to be less control. And as we grow, as we learn, we will increasingly become more aware of when trust is required and when control is required. It is finding the balance that shows a strong connection and understands that aspects of our destinies are not in our control.

October 17

"Only trust can bring tomorrow."

t's only when we trust that the knowing exists that the sun will rise tomorrow and that the day will have a dawn and a sunset. It is this trust that must be abundant in our lives because when there is fear and anxiety, tomorrow will always remain far away. The future is not found in fear, and it's only when trust is called upon that tomorrow delivers our destinies. When we escape our fearful programming that our egos create, the beauty of our inner self shows the trust required to fulfill our purposes.

October 18

"The first lesson of trust is patience."

The best way we can test our trust is by understanding patience. Patience requires that we have a deep-seated understanding and an intense belief that converts trust into patience that is not accompanied by anxiety or fear. That trust grows because we are patient, and we are patient when we trust with no fear or anxiety.

October 19

"Reasoning brings us logic. Trust gives us purpose."

t's a known fact that we must always strive to understand our daily tasks, our functions in this world. We require the reasoning of our egos to give us the logic that makes us understand our choices, our decisions, and our positions in the world. When we embark on projects with passion, we find the reasoning to give that logic, but the trust gives us the purpose. Logic does not come from the soul but it is a fundamental requirement that grows trust and allows us the wisdom of our purposes. When we combine reasoning and trust, we find that wisdom flows through every task—and we grow in the knowledge of tomorrow. Logic and purpose are sometimes far apart, but the soul, through a strong connection to the ego, binds them and brings reasoning and trust to fulfill our lessons.

October 20

*"Don't let your ego color your path
with a negative cloud."*

Anxiety breeds fear and stops us from moving forward. It's the biggest signpost from our egos to take us to a wall of fear. We must overcome and find our souls' guidance; that will lead us through trust and fill our paths with positive gratefulness. We can only counter anxiety through the understanding and wisdom of trust. When we are on our paths, we are given so much, but we must trust forever. Don't fill your path with a negative cloud because you will never see the beauty of the dawn or the colors of a sunset.

Patience

It's in the moments that are long
in those ones that linger,
it's then that we require patience
that brings the understanding and not the fear.

For it's in the moments that are long
that cause the frustration because they have no end.
But it's in the moments, those long moments,
that we will learn the most.

For as we grow, we must find that patience
is not only a virtue,
but it definitely is a passage to wisdom.

For the more we rush,
the more we lose the quietness that shows the beauty,
the peacefulness that brings the reward,
the understanding that displays the wisdom.

For it's about the journey, and not its completion.
For it's in those moments, those long moments
that make us discover the journey and its beauty,
and not just rushing to its conclusion.

October 21

"It takes infinite patience in finding wisdom."

The world we live in is one where the here and now is most important. Immediate resolution and gratification are everything in our lives. People postpone the stories of their souls, and they require immediate solutions to the quests of the ego. The soul often reveals the path only for us to say, "We are not ready now. We will tell you when we are ready." Our souls become patient, and they wait for our connections to happen. The biggest lesson about patience is that it brings wisdom. We require infinite patience. For then, we are living close to our souls.

October 22

"Patience requires hard work."

t often feels as though we are drifting along, expecting answers. During these phases, we tell ourselves to wait patiently. We must never mistake it with doing nothing, and we must understand that patience requires us to get ready to grow. Patience is not something we intend; it is moments of quietness that allow us to focus and rid ourselves of all the things we don't require. Someone with patience focuses on worldly events with the soulful meaning to understanding them. It is the process and the understanding that everything happens when we are ready, but it requires that we do the work to make us ready.

October 23

"Patience must always overcome pride."

t is through patience that we learn and grow. Pride is the ego's way of creating fear, creating self-importance, and stopping growth. It is important that we allow the soul's patience to shine through to understand the lessons and slowly lead us in growth. Patience is the ever-important factor in awareness. Awareness happens when we are patient and not when we are trying to show our self-importance and fight against the lessons because of pride. Patience allows us acceptance. It shows us the options, and it makes us aware.

October 24

"Tempering a sword requires time and patience."

You, as the blacksmith of your life, must temper your existence as you would temper a sword to make it strong and useful. We don't necessarily understand what happens during the tempering process, but we need to know that the process brings us skill, knowledge, and wisdom to extract the most in the deliverance of our purposes. It requires time and patience, and as the blacksmith knows, impatience and shortcuts force faults and weak spots in the metal and cause it to break. As the blacksmith of your life, embrace time and accept patience. Live joyfully, in the moment, knowing that the wisdom you are acquiring will make you strong. Temper yourself through time and patience.

October 25

"Patience is a long-term view with short-term results."

Growth and transformation happen regardless of what we intend. All we can do is be aware and listen closely to ensure that our growth, our transformation, occurs on our paths—and that we aren't growing and transforming off our paths with no purpose. To have patience in life means we have peace, we are settled, and we understand that tomorrow is a result of what we do today. Yet we can't get to tomorrow before completing today. Patience understands that tranquility, that peacefulness we find when we believe that our paths are lined with all the beauty we require. When we have that peacefulness, that understanding, and that patience, we find joy, we become positive, and we find the short-term result that brings meaning to our lives. Patience requires vision.

Forgetfulness

We often are so intent on finding reasons to fight
that we forget to see all the reasons to love.
Our focus on the world must move away
from self-centeredness toward a humble acceptance
of the grace and love we have.

For our positions in this world
are often about finding fault
to prove who we are, to show that we are right.
And it's through that process
that we grow our egos,
that we hurt our souls.

For it's through love and through humbleness
where we are less,
that we find true acceptance of ourselves
and our meaning to this world.

October 26

*"Don't forget what you need to remember—and
don't remember what you need to forget."*

Life is filled with stages. There are moments of discomfort
and despair, and there are moments of joy and gratefulness.
We must not dwell on the things in the past that bring us
fear and anxiety. We must learn to forget and start afresh on
the intended path. We must also not forget the lessons we have
learned and all the wisdom we have gained. It is a matter of focus.
It is a matter of understanding importance.

October 27

"Forgetfulness can be the ego's greatest beauty."

Self-importance, fear, anxiety, and all the issues that the ego uses to control our lives make us—and force us to become—*soul removed*. The ego's greatest beauty must be when that connectedness to the soul becomes a strong force and forgetfulness sets in to replace the self-importance, the fear, and the anxiety. Egotistical humbleness will always win the day because it allows the soul to shine, give light, and show the way. Forgetfulness is our greatest beauty.

October 28

*"Remember that your blessings are
bigger than any bad periods."*

We often fall into the spiral of the *wrong forgetfulness*. The wrong forgetfulness implies that we forget everything that is positive, everything our souls give to us, and all the blessings we receive from God, and we only focus on the negative. This is the *ego's forgetfulness*. It distracts through negative thoughts. It stops us growing because we fear and expect the worst. So, everything must be tainted with that negative thought, the wrong forgetfulness. The right forgetfulness forgets our importance and forgets that we need this worldly stature to find happiness. We forget ourselves onto greatness. Happiness is found in trust and freedom—and not through the forgetfulness of our blessings, our lives, and our purposeful paths. Count your blessings every day for they far exceed the negatives of any bad periods.

"In seeking self-importance, we rarely find our true importance."

t must be said that the egotistical search for our destinies often leads to a life filled with empty regrets. We must allow our souls to connect and drive our egos in search of our true importance. True importance can only really be seen through the eyes of others—beyond our own vision of a self-centered and somewhat happy existence. Our dreams must be the ones that don't see volume; they must see substance. That doesn't know importance, but it understands faith. That remembers tomorrow because it is forgetful of yesterday. Our importance is to see ourselves through other's eyes; therein lies our delivery of purpose.

October 30

"It is the moments of forgetfulness that makes us shine."

When we decide to forget our own importance, our own opinions, and our own control, our souls' beauty is revealed to the world. We are great at hiding that beauty behind the high walls of egotistical behavior. So, remember the moments of forgetfulness and make them more because that is what makes us shine.

October 31

"Be grateful for all the small victories over yourself."

Overcoming yourself, forgetting yourself, is an accomplishment that needs the ego's acknowledgment. These victories allow our purposes to shine through. They clear the clouds and display our destinies. They bring the sunshine to our lives and brightly illuminate our paths and our positions among others. Forgetting ourselves is a victory that never can stand alone, but it will always be the continuous quest to overcome and stand victorious every day because we know we have won. It is not the single event; it is a continuous soul-fulfilling journey. We must be grateful, and we must understand these victories because that is what grows us.

"Memories are of people who glow not because they think they are somebody, but they have become somebody to themselves—and ultimately somebody to the world."

To make memories, you must become somebody for yourself. Only then will you have value to the world. It's only when you decide that you don't want to be somebody that you become somebody. When you decide you don't want to be on the who's who list, you make the all-important list. It is not about fame and fortune; it's about finding your tracks. The wonderful thing about a train is that it can only travel on tracks; if you want to be on destiny's path, be like a train on tracks. If there are no tracks there, don't go there. Finding yourself, finding that you are somebody, is actually about finding your tracks.

*"Once you give the world its freedom, you
will surely find your own freedom."*

Forgetting yourself has more to do with the world around you than with yourself. As long as the ego needs to control the world, we will battle with forgetting ourselves. Controlling the world around us keeps us captive and stops us from enjoying the freedom that trust brings to our lives. To give the world its freedom means doing the work and not insisting on the outcome. We can only find true freedom when we allow the world its own freedom. When the ego lets go of control, the soul takes charge of our purposes.

November 3

"Think of yourself—but only through others."

When you think less of yourself, it's only because of the ego's programming. When you think more of yourself, it's only because of the ego's programming. It is very important to think of yourself through others. Access yourself by understanding your value, by what you bring to the world and to the other souls you touch. Thinking of yourself through others is the soul's way of forcing the ego to forget itself and remember the inner value that one is all about. We must always understand that if there is a difference between how we see ourselves and how others see us, it's the high walls that the ego erected through programming and creating fear, self-doubt, and a lack of awareness. It is imperative that we see the difference and access ourselves as often as we can through the way that others see us.

"Happiness is in what we see and in what we feel—and not in what we have or want."

The power of forgetfulness is to take us from our egos to our souls, make us see the pictures that surround us, and fill us with beauty and hope. It makes us feel the power of our souls. It allows us to forget the fears and the anxiety our egos feed off of. Our gratitude, therefore, should be in the things we see and feel—and not in the things we want. The danger of the ego is to always postpone happiness. To make it another step before you reach it. It will always ask for more before happiness can be attained. Happiness needs forgetfulness because there is always something of more beauty in what we are than in what the ego thinks we need.

Surrender

Surrender your mind,
then your soul will triumph.
But you have to surrender your soul
to allow your path to be revealed.

Surrendering of our minds
means committing to our souls.
It means that we have to allow
our hearts to show the way.

It's that wisdom that we need,
but we have to surrender our hearts
to that fountain of wisdom, hand it over,
to a body strong and filled with knowledge.

And then we have to connect
through the soul to that wisdom.
Surrendering the mind requires
a surrender of the heart.

November 5

*"Being true to yourself has got nothing
to do with negotiation and control; it has
everything to do with listening."*

D on't replace programming with other wrong programming.
You don't have negotiating power with the soul. The soul
doesn't negotiate. You can't bargain with God. You need
to accept all the wonder of what is on your path. Everything—the
good and the bad—has some value. It's about surrender. It is not
about negotiation and control; it is about listening and accepting.

November 6

"Surrender to your soul's wisdom."

The block for progress is often control. We stop our wisdom from shining through because we control and need to be in control of every facet of our lives. This control obstructs our progress because it is egotistical and needs the outside to conform while we do not conform to our inside. Inner strength is built on the surrendering values of our egos and our souls to the wisdom that we have been given. It is important that we surrender and hand control over so that our souls can guide us and lead the way in wisdom and trust.

"True surrender is the manifestation of wisdom."

To surrender is a state of being that is a condition of willingly understanding our purposes. It comes about through the knowledge and growth of all the lessons we have learned—of all the obstacles we have bridged—and it shows itself through the wisdom of our daily actions. Surrender has no memory; it has a knowing that realizes the potential of our paths. It hands over control, and it plans with the soul for certainty. Surrender is the wisdom in all of us.

"Forgetting your ego leads to surrendering your soul."

Discovering your path requires an awareness that starts with a forgetfulness of oneself. It is when we get into understanding of forgetfulness of our egos that we expose our paths and open the door to our souls. Surrender is not about the ego. It calls for our souls, our inner strength, to surrender to our purposes, our paths, and our destinies. Forgetting ourselves onto greatness is removing the obstacles of our egos and enabling our souls to surrender. Surrender is a gift. It is a growth that cannot be understood; it can only be experienced. It brings a wisdom. It is visibly seen through the energy and the being of the person. Surrender is the smile of God in humanity.

"When you surrender your will, you don't
lose it; you just find the right one."

We find every possible way to enforce our will, our control, and our purposes on the lives we lead. We find the insecurity of our own will and control brings us very shallow emotional comfort. We think that our will, our control, makes us safe. The opposite is true. When we lose our will and lose control, we find that control through purpose is something of true meaning and guidance. Surrendering our will doesn't mean we escape anxiety, but it does mean that anxiety makes us grow. When we surrender control, it doesn't mean we trust blindly, but we trust because we know our purposes. When we surrender our fear, it doesn't mean we become self-centered, but it does mean we become soulful. Our will is linked to controlling our environments, and all we need is to surrender our will and accept our purposes.

Gratitude

There must be time for rest,
time for relaxation,
and time for prayer.

For it's in those times of quiet meditation
that we fill our minds with the energy,
a soulful peacefulness,
that comes directly from our hearts.

There must be a time to relax and reflect
not on our daily tasks,
but on the discovery of the other parts
that brings fullness to our journey.

There must be a time to comprehend
and understand the beauty of it all.
But most important,
there must always be a time to be thankful
for all the blessings we get.

For it's those times that mean the most
and that will carry us over the mountains
and through the valleys.
There must be a time to be grateful.

November 10

"Right now, in this moment, be thankful."

t's our nature, it's the ego's ability, to find the unhappiness and create the fear, but right now, find the things to be grateful for. See the joys, the grace, around you, and that will bring your soul to your thoughts. Be happy, and tomorrow will be happier. For what we think, the origin of our thoughts, will be our disposition in the future. So, find something to be grateful for. There is so much. You will find that you don't have to wait any longer because happiness, joy, and wisdom exist right now.

November 11

"Gratitude is the salt and pepper of life."

As salt and pepper bring taste and flavor to food, being grateful brings joy and understanding to life. It's the grace of this world—the things we don't see or don't understand—that we must be grateful for. Through our souls, we open that window and allow the wind to blow gratefulness into our lives. When we understand the joys we have and the beauty that exists, more can be revealed. The soul brings clarity to life, but it is in being grateful that we reward the grace we are given.

November 12

"Just think—and then say thank you."

As humans, we have the unique ability to be grateful, but we also find self-importance in our gratitude. We don't need to sift through all our blessings to find the important ones to be thankful for. Blessings are of equal stature—no matter how big or small. We do, however, need to focus on the real blessings of importance that build to our purposes and help us fulfill our destinies. In these blessings, gratitude and thankfulness somehow seem like not enough. They erase our self-importance and make us forget ourselves and become the small soulful individual with each one of our enormous purposes. It is important to think, to ponder, and then just say thank you.

Presence

Remember the moment
remember the day.
For gifts are given
that must still be unwrapped.

For love is always present
that must still be accepted.
For there is beauty in every day
that we must still get ourselves to see.

Remember the moment
remember the day.
For growth is a process that starts
at the beginning of each day.

We grow in our lessons
we discover our wisdom
we forget our egos
and start living in our souls.

We age in beauty
we deliver our purposes
and we find all this
takes a mere second.

November 13

"Yesterday only matters when it can correct today."

Don't live in the past or allow the past to be alive in you today. The lessons we learn are the only important aspects of yesterday. They help us find tomorrow in a better way. Our programming and all the mistakes we have made bring insight and understanding that make us teachers in many ways. Evolution grows through us and makes our souls discover the wisdom on our paths. The process of yesterday makes our choices better today.

November 14

"Treasure today."

We must live as though today is the only day that matters. To truly live is to live in a forgetful way. Accepting our paths is all about treasuring today. The past has come and gone, and our choices and decisions cannot be changed, but what we have ahead of us starts with today. Our thoughts, our paths, and our destinies are always there and will be guided by what we do today. Treasure today because yesterday is gone—and today is the start of tomorrow.

November 15

"Don't let tomorrow spoil the beauty of today."

Dreams, goals, and plans are the cornerstones of our paths in this world. We must remember not to let tomorrow's plans spoil our progress today. It is a bit of a two-way street; the one requires the other, and for us to go in a direction, we need to think of tomorrow, but if thinking of tomorrow brings fear and anxiety to today, it is defeating what we intend to achieve. It is important that we think of tomorrow and plan for tomorrow knowing we have the ability, the confidence, the trust, and the belief that bring the beauty to our plans today. When we surrender our dreams and our goals, we don't bring the fear and the anxiety of tomorrow to us today.

*"Joy and happiness are often revealed through
our attitudes about the present."*

We are but human with emotions and moods. Our attitudes reveal our commitments to our lives, to our journeys, and to our purposes. Joy, happiness, and the fulfillment of our purposes must always be in harmony with our attitudes about the present moment—no matter how difficult or unclear. Our attitudes about the present must trust our souls' biggest purpose. It must accept that guidance comes from within, and it must keep us focused on the positive. There will always be those who drag us to negativity, try intercept our attitudes, and take us away from our focus on our purposes and destinies. Our commitment is therefore revealed through our attitudes about the present moment because that grounds us and brings us happiness and joy.

November 17

"To reach tomorrow, you have to complete today."

Reaching our dreams is about the fulfillment of moments. It is about the momentum and the energy of growth today. We have to learn and complete our lessons. We have to overcome our obstacles to understand the meaning of tomorrow. The energy of today brings the dream ever closer. The more we work at understanding tomorrow, the sooner it comes.

November 18

"Let yesterday guide your tomorrow."

Life is made up of lessons learned, programming corrected, and memories that make us who we are. It is important that the lessons we learn today, the programming we correct, and the memories we make guide us to tomorrow. Every day is the start of the new opportunity to learn our lessons, to program, and to leave others with pleasant memories. Therefore, what we do today will guide us tomorrow.

*"We must live in the moment and not
bring our pasts to the moment."*

To grow and evolve, it is important that we respond to the moment and not to the past through the moment. To resolve the fears and the anxiety our egos created, we must let go of the past. To establish a future that is filled with growth, we must respond to the moment. We must gather the knowledge. We must prosper in confidence. To do this, the moment requires the wisdom from our souls. Let us not give in to the illusion created by fear and anxiety that can only see threats and danger in any moment, limiting our growth and evolution. Let us see beyond the past and deliver tomorrow with the confidence of today.

Focus

It's the focus that gets us to relax.
It's that focus that brings us the trust.
For the more we live through wisdom,
the clearer our paths become.

Walking slowly feels like nothing is happening.
Patience brings us to a feeling of passivity.
We want to run.

But it is in the difficult times that we need to understand
that lessons are only learned through temporary upheavals.
We only make these problems last
Because in the moment we don't trust,
and we want to fight.

It's that calmness that we need.
It's that process that takes us
to faith and understanding.
That is why the temporary upheavals exist.

So, make them temporary,
understand your patience,
and walk slowly with focus and awareness.

Do not fear.
For everything is guided.
Even our disappointments.

If we are on our paths, and if we remain steadfast,
the disappointments are those temporary moments
where wisdom was needed
but ego was found.

November 20

"Always be spiritually productive."

For us to grow and to develop, we need to be spiritually productive. This productivity requires all our awareness to seek and find our lessons at every possible opportunity. It requires us to work hard at helping others in their searches, and our impact can only be positive if our productivity is high. Spiritual productivity requires that we search from within but deliver an awareness that is noticed from the outside. Every day be spiritually productive, and joy will find its way to you.

"Our responsibilities can be our greatest joy."

When we live in balance—and we live in the soul—the possibilities are endless, but there are great responsibilities. When we discover all these endless possibilities, we accept responsibility for them and realize that the responsibility is no burden. Walking toward our destinies is an absolute joy. Possibilities equal responsibilities in the same way as balance equals the soul.

November 22

"Discover the fun in discipline."

Teach the world—shout it out. The biggest fun, the greatest joy, can be found in the security of discipline. It's our egos that want the freedom. They want to explore, but our souls know the way and understand the wisdom we have. Our souls need the discipline—and the time and the security—to show the way. The more chaos our egos enact, the bigger the obstacles. The greater the wall, the more difficult it is for our souls to lead us on the path. Discipline brings fun because it calms us and gives us joy in the knowledge that we know our paths and trust our destinies. That is when what is within becomes what is without.

November 23

"Being in service of our souls requires perseverance."

We must never think that our souls' paths, our journeys of purpose, are an easy stroll, free of any obstacles and problems. When we walk our paths, when we are in service of our souls, we require constant thought, constant spiritual guidance, and a constant block from fear and egotistical anxieties. There are so many easier ways, so many convincing ways, that bring our egos to control and take us along those paths. The soul's journey is about lessons learned, growth in ourselves, growing others, touching lives, the whispering of hope, the teachings of destiny, and the acceptance of our own journeys. It is important that we understand the service to our souls requires hard work and dedication because the task never ends, but it does get easier.

November 24

"Don't forget to rest because that's
when you work the hardest."

It is in the downtime, the holidays, that our spirits find the most value, action, and connection with our egos. When we rest and remove the daily burdens of work and the associated stress of the world, we free our hearts to show their dreams. When we relax, our egos drop their guard and allow the connection with our hearts to become stronger. Make time to rest. The more we spend quality time with our souls, the better we fulfill our duties.

November 25

"Spiritual freedom often requires worldly detention."

Finding the freedom to allow our souls to escape and deliver our purposes requires the discipline to abstain from everything that detracts and takes us off our paths. We must often detain ourselves to find the silence, the peace, to escape the world and seek clarity through our souls. It is something we must teach; it is something that is expected of us to show. It is a leader's greatest quality because when leaders focus on spiritual freedom, their souls grow. They are locked away from the worldly events that can alter their paths. As we grow, this freedom opens up more and more. Sometimes we must tell people to lock themselves up in order to gain freedom.

November 26

*"First do what you have to do—and
then what you want to do."*

When we lead with our souls, our tasks, our purposes become very guided. It requires that we do and fulfill the tasks at hand. The ego takes us off to do things from the egotistical center, tries to govern through fear, and leads us off our paths through pleasure. Our souls need us to do the things we need to do because they are important. The small things require the most input, but the big things change through the guidance of the soul.

"Inspiration is often in application."

Our hearts want us to act. They want to show us, and our minds want to stop us and hold us in fear. We search for perfection and try to find what our minds tell us must be there, but the greatest things happen when we allow the soul to apply itself to the task. When that freedom reigns through creating, bringing together, and applying the wisdom of our souls, the inspiration feeds the lonely mind. It removes those fearful barriers of what is right and what is best, and it allows the application to overcome the search.

Gifts of the Heart

Rewards of Path

Divinity

Our strength is about becoming one
in heart and mind.
Believe in what we hoped for
and have faith in what we cannot see.

For the dreams become the miracles,
and that is what should rule this world.

For when we accept the miracle of our existence
And understand the depth of our dreams,
we are able to change in ourselves
and through that, change the world.

The stronger we are in mind and soul,
the bigger our impact,
the stronger our growth.

"Miracles have no reason and need no debate."

When we challenge our faith, it does not mean that we don't believe. It only means that we doubt and therefore have no faith. The miracle of life cannot be reasoned out or debated by us thinking we can come up with answers that make sense. All we need is spiritual guidance to follow the process that leads us to an understanding that needs very little intervention—and a lot more faith.

November 29

"Focus on the unseen because it makes
what is seen so much clearer."

What we see and what we touch often limits our enjoyment and the beauty of life. It narrows our perspectives of our paths and our souls' wisdom. It is the egotistical approach that needs control, that needs to see and touch, and that understands only what the ego finds of value. The true beauty of life is in what we can't see and what we can't touch. This widens our spiritual perspective on life. It allows our souls the freedom to soar. It shows us a clear path, it gives us wisdom, and it ultimately makes us understand that what is seen is temporary, but what is unseen becomes eternal. Focus on what is not seen—and you will see everything clearer.

November 30

"Don't cover your miracles in clouds of anxiousness."

Anxiety, fear, and a lack of trust often block the revelation of all the gifts and blessings we can receive. They stop us from walking into a cloud because we are forever asking for a light, a compass, or a tower that will guide our paths. Sometimes all we require is trusting the hand that leads us. It leads us through any cloud of fear, and the more we grow, the bigger our confidence becomes in searching for the miracles that are hidden on our paths.

December 1

"Joy is what we give, and it should never be confused with what we receive because what we receive is grace."

We must live with balance and harmony that reflects the beauty of our souls, and that will be defined as joy by other people. What we receive from other people when we live in a state of balance is ultimately the gift of grace. It's only then that we truly understand that we are here to give and not to receive. Receiving is a gift, and we should be grateful for that. Living in a giving way is about joy. So, what do we give? We give in trust, we give ourselves, and we ultimately must give our souls in the service of our paths and our destinies to become what we should be. So, joy is about giving and not receiving.

December 2

"Miracles are beyond the control of our fear and anxiety."

We must understand that the miracles in our lives are not because of our own control. They are really a gift. The true meaning and gratitude must therefore be found in the way we accept. We cannot make them or control them; our fear and anxiety have no effect on them. They are beyond our control. During these processes, we must find focus and discipline. That is all we need to make the miracle happen, but that is the ultimate form of control. When we are sidetracked, we forget about the control that is required to make the miracle happen, and often that is when it happens. Control becomes obstructive when it is driven by fear, anxiety, or our obsession with understanding and growing. Miracles are beyond our control.

December 3

"If you don't see the miracle, how
can you ever be thankful?"

I f you go through life not being aware of the large miracles and the small ones—the seasons changing is a miracle—how can you be thankful? How can you have that gratitude in your soul that you keep bottled up because it wants to leap out in joy? We allow our egos to lead the way in fear and anxiety with absolutely no knowledge or awareness of the miracles that are given to us. Be aware of the miracle, be thankful, and be grateful—and your soul will soar.

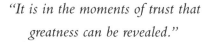

December 4

*"It is in the moments of trust that
greatness can be revealed."*

We often ask ourselves why greatness through the universe cannot be shown to us in a clear and concise manner, but somehow that defeats our purpose because greatness is always present. We only choose not to trust its revelation. In these moments of trust, true greatness will be revealed because we believe and acknowledge God's presence. It is important to trust so that greatness can be delivered. What has this got to do with it? The answer is simple. When we stand at the point where the miracle will be achieved—when we sit at the precipice of greatness—we must understand how calm and peaceful trust makes us feel. That is the moment when greatness can really be delivered.

December 5

"Waiting for the miracle means you are not being aware."

The ego will always convince us that our ship must come in. The ego will always soar to see the beauty and not wait to find a place to land. Our lives cannot be held at ransom by our egos professing knowledge and wisdom. Like the eagle soars, we must allow our souls the freedom of flight without the fear of not knowing where to land. That requires trust in understanding that it will show itself when it is ready. Waiting for the miracle means we are missing all the miracles in between. If we are not soaring, we are focused on what we believe is true. Waiting for the miracle reflects an unawareness, and a miracle can only happen when we acknowledge all the other miracles.

December 6

"Your life should be art—and there is an art to your life."

From the day we enter this world, we have the canvas to create the masterpiece that can fill the foyer of this wonderful world we live in. With all the masterpieces hanging, we can walk from room to room, through the passages of time, and draw the wisdom from all that has been here before us and give them to those yet to come. As we create our masterpieces, we must fill them with the colors and textures that create the warmth and the depth of understanding that all of us are blessed with. We must break the shackles of the darkness that we are so easily attracted to. We must cleanse the doubtful energy that sits on our shoulders, ready to pounce when the soul reveals its purpose. This masterpiece, this art that we call life, reflects our humble understanding of where tomorrow will lead us and the trust we understand. We will frame this masterpiece when it is time to let go. When we stand there gazing at its beauty, we never feel regret, doubt, or fear because during our lives, we are given chances to erase that and correct the imperfections that stop us from filling this canvas with our true beauty, our true reason, and our purpose for those yet to come. Life is art, but there is an art to life.

December 7

"Crossing over means coming together."

The awakening we find in people's lives becomes the pinnacle, sometimes a moment, where they understand that they have crossed over. They have stepped over a line in the sand, acknowledging that the connectedness to their soul is more important than their position in the world. When we step over that line, when we cross over and acknowledge that deeper understanding, we come together, but this can never be a miracle in a second. For this miracle develops over time because it brings forgetfulness, passion, and clear vision of the path and the way yet to come. The more we accept this purpose, the greater our understanding becomes. All the different facets of our existence come together and unite in this one common cause. Identifying that common cause can be the miracle of a lifetime, but when we are lucky, it can be seen in a moment—and explored in a lifetime.

Wisdom

Why do we search for what we already have?

A life's journey is filled
with climbing the highest mountains,
overcoming the biggest burdens,
all in search for what our minds tell us we need.

We look for answers in far places.
We look for joy and happiness
in all the wrong places.

Yet when we find our guiding hand,
we will discover its presence
was always there.

For we need not search too far.
We need not try to find what we already know
and can discover through a peaceful and quiet trust.

For it's there, inside us.
It's hidden in our souls.

And the more we connect with it,
the clearer it becomes,
revealing the answers
and the wisdom our minds so need.

It's that forgetfulness, that quiet peacefulness,
that makes our lives full of wisdom,
filled with confidence
and the understanding and trust
that will give us a future of purpose.

December 8

"Wisdom is never momentary thoughts—it comes through discovery of our purposes."

We must never search for wisdom because it cannot be found. Wisdom finds us when we discover our paths and our reasons for being. Wisdom makes us bigger, and it clears our thoughts, our barriers, to program better. Wisdom allows us the opportunity to grow while programming ourselves and others in a clear and constructive way. Wisdom is not easily granted, and it requires us to work at fulfilling our purposes. Wisdom can easily be taken away when we lose our way or fall off our paths. Never see wisdom as a fleeting thought but rather as the result of a purpose-driven path.

December 9

"Wisdom is more about silence than about noise."

Egotistical, noisy behavior is remarkably effective in hiding the soul's beauty. Wisdom knows when to be quiet, always listens, and will only act when the true opportunity presents itself. When wisdom speaks, everybody knows. When wisdom shows the way, everybody will follow. Wisdom does not prove importance. It does not judge. It does not want rewards. It only shows the way by giving the lesson and providing the warmth that creates a future. So, let us find our souls and deliver the wisdom, not through noisy behavior but through quiet contemplation, reflection, and leadership when required.

*"Wisdom shows us how little we know. The
more we grow, the more we pray."*

When we grow in wisdom, the reflection in the mirror shows us how little control we have over our purposes and our lives beyond. The wiser we get, the more we realize our reliance on prayer, thought, and meditation. The wiser we get, the less need we have for control. Growth comes from the place where control is not required. Where wisdom leads, trust shows our paths and gives us the answers to the lessons we learn. The wiser we get, the less we know. The less we know, the more we pray—and the wiser we get.

"Vision doesn't happen in a moment."

Wisdom collected will eventually shine through to show us direction. Vision is not brilliance of the moment; it is brilliance over ages. It requires that we fulfill our purposes, that we learn our lessons, and that we listen to reason. We must find the leadership of our souls to guide us through wisdom to a clear vision. It is how we start that makes the day. For everything must have a beginning. Ensure that the beginning of everything comes from the vision of light and wisdom—and not from darkness and negativity. Vision does not happen in the moment.

December 12

"Your wisdom will always find a way."

The difference in being wise and thinking from within can only be understood when we realize that any problem can be solved if our thinking comes from within. The barriers we erect as defenses for the threats that our egos perceive are often nothing more than a mirage in the desert, but when we muster our forces from within, our wisdom will deliver the true picture and not a mirage of fear and self-doubt. Wisdom is harnessed in every one of us.

December 13

"Wisdom is not in a thought. It's more in a feeling."

When we live our lives knowing—and when we live our lives with the awareness of knowledge—we find the peace that calms the restlessness and overcomes the fear. When we live our lives knowing we have the confidence, we clear the barriers because we know, and that is because the wisdom within us has no boundaries. It knows no obstacles for it understands tomorrow, and it sees the road ahead. Wisdom is the knowing we have, and it is not the thoughts we create.

December 14

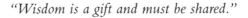

"Wisdom is a gift and must be shared."

Every day we are given more wisdom, a better understanding, and a clearer vision of our paths, our hearts, and our souls. It is up to us to create the awareness to see this unfold and to make it part of our daily tasks, through which we discover our purposes and paths. This awareness must always be present, and we must not allow our egos to block it. If it does, we lose the opportunity to gather the wisdom and share it with the world.

December 15

"Calmness is not a lack of—it's an abundance of."

The quietness and calmness of a spiritual being reflects an understanding, a wisdom, that comes from within. It is that wisdom that shows that rationality can only be a part of spirituality when we understand the connection between our souls and our egos. It is that amazement that things do happen, not just through our doing but mostly through understanding and trust. When we find that calmness, it shows an abundance of wisdom and connection. It needs very little because we know that value comes from our souls—and not necessarily from our egos or this world.

"Wisdom never shows experience.
It only reveals progress."

The first lesson in wisdom is that it does not come from experience. No intellect or theory brings it. No thought or egotistical search will reveal it. Wisdom shows itself through the forgetful nature of our egos when our souls are leading the way. On our paths, we make progress. On our paths, our souls grow to show greater understanding. So, wisdom is revealed when we have gained the understanding required to fulfill the next step of our journeys. Our souls will impart wisdom to help others progress, but we must never try to show our wisdom because that is egotistical and wrong. Wisdom shows itself with no intervention from the ego.

"Wisdom is like cookies; having them all
at once gives you a sore tummy."

Our method of living is about losing the fear and anxiety we are born into. Our method of living depends on how we discover the wisdom that bring us freedom, but too much wisdom can confuse us. Knowledge needs to be interspersed with practical applications to grow and find the next bit even more rewarding. Our method of living cannot be about finding all the answers right now; it is about evolving and discovering the right answer for this moment. Do not go in search of all the wisdom at once; that will confuse and unbalance you. Wisdom is like cookies. Your life's wisdom will always stay in the cookie jar—and only you can remove it, piece by piece. You can enjoy it because that is growth and understanding.

December 18

"Never deny yourself moments of wisdom."

Our frustrations, our fears, and our negative mindsets often are the cause of denying the wisdom our guides impart to us in every moment of the day. We block this wisdom because we find reasons to. The reasons are of no importance, but egotistical outings make us feel we are in control. Wisdom is not in the answers; it is the clear and clever path of bringing us joy, fulfilling our lives, and experiencing the gratitude we have for being here. Wisdom opens doors and closes the ones we don't need. Don't let negative thoughts, frustrations, or fear deny you the possibilities of life. Wisdom can guide us through them all.

December 19

"Don't expect wisdom to creep up and surprise you."

We often want to be surprised. We have a need to be entertained, but to be wise, to understand, is about past experiences. It is about seeing, through awareness, the purpose of what is done. When we don't understand, we accept that one day we will. Wisdom grows as we become more like we should. It grows when we become purposeful in our lives. To be wise is both a blessing and hard work because it calls for awareness that must be understood. Be aware and understand that surprises will always be there through the awareness of the experiences in our lives.

December 20

"Let your mind age in the riches of your soul's wisdom."

As good wine matures in oak, we must allow our lives to mature through the wisdom of our hearts. When we live through our egos, we lack the depth and understanding that our hearts, our souls, give us. We live in the moment, and we seek beauty in a way that reflects an egotistical need for strength and position. When we live through our hearts, we see beauty that reflects the wisdom of time. It need not show its stature or importance because it is just beauty on its own. Maturity through the heart brings wisdom to our lives.

December 21

"When wisdom flows, faith grows."

Faith grows when wisdom flows because it is required to be the strength behind the quest for destiny. Understanding that we require knowledge and wisdom for faith to become stronger is part of the discovery process. The ego will always place barriers of self-doubt, no confidence, and fear in the way. That obstructs the flow of wisdom and knowledge and stops our faith from growing. Wisdom flows when faith grows, which means that the stronger our faith becomes, the more wisdom is revealed. The less we allow the ego to obstruct and block, the more we learn—and the clearer our paths. So, allow wisdom to flow as our faith grows—and believe that our faith grows when wisdom flows.

Love

Even if you deny all the truths of your soul,
if you refuse to understand
the impact of your soul in this world,
where does love come from?

What is love if it is not
the deepest, the greatest, outpour
of the soul's purpose?

We can refuse to acknowledge
that our souls exist
and that we have a purpose,
and spend our lives in disbelief
for we live every day as a gamble.

When we discover love in a child, or for another,
it comes from a spiritual well
that can't be found in our minds
or through philosophy of some kind.

Love exposes our souls,
and it forces us to discover
the deeper meaning of our being.

And we realize that love is not in a thought,
but it is compacted in the deepest crevice
of the knowledge of our souls.

*"The purpose of growth is to learn
and understand our paths."*

This growth leads to love. Love makes us understand our environments, our world, and the other souls around us. This love is a gift. It is trust and faith captured and can be shown through our daily actions. This love transcends all our egotistical fears, it gives us peace, and it forms a calmness that shows we trust and don't treat everything with suspicion or egotistical anxiety. It transcends our programming. It corrects our beliefs. It makes us the beings we are meant to be. In the moments when we grow, we will use all we have to understand the lesson. Sometimes we object or fight, but through love and God's willingness, we are shown the way.

December 23

"Love blossoms through awareness."

Awareness makes our love grow. It fills our souls with the hope and guidance for tomorrow. Self-importance and egotistical ways make our love die. When we find that, the awareness gives us momentum—and we find the wisdom hidden in love. Wisdom comes directly from our souls and shows the beauty of us—and of those around us. It leads us to make the right choices. It holds us and guides us to blossom because our souls are leading our processions. Love is all about awareness.

December 24

"Unconditional love is the soul's gift to the ego."

We discover unconditional love when we find that source of peace and surrender that makes something else more important than us. That is the gift our souls give our egos, and that leads them to forgetfulness, which leads them to surrender—and the loss of all the fear and anxiety associated with this world. Unconditional love becomes our biggest growth because our purpose is to find, not through who we are or what we do but by single-minded focus to deliver our purposes and evolve, creating a better place and making our connectedness abundantly clear. When our egos find this gift, it often, and sometimes with force, surrenders to the purpose of our souls.

December 25

"Love is the answer—and it's always with us."

No matter how troublesome or filled with problems a life can be, the answer is to fill the problems, to fill the fears, and to fill the anxieties with little pockets of love. Love is always present. When we make decisions, our choices can be based on egotistical theory or soulful love. When we connect, we find that we are filled with love. It remains the strongest connection, and it has boundless beauty to deliver the true message on a path that leads to destiny, which is all love.

December 26

"Love always fills the potholes in our paths."

Through reprogramming and discovery, we slowly evolve with our purposes, our paths, and our destinies in mind. We discover our potholes, and that is what makes us evolve through the lessons that we need to progress further. A very important—and ultimately the most important—aspect in our lives is the discovery of love. Love is the gift we receive. It is not the ego's love; it is the love that exists from God to humanity. That is the love that allows us to heal and grow in peace. It is this love, this deep inner love, that fills our potholes of the past and makes us give more to the world. It is the love that exists from a parent to a child, and ultimately, it is stronger than anything known to humanity.

December 27

"Let love empty you of yourself."

We often need to empty the bucket and fill it with fresh water. We need to sit and view the world through new eyes. We need to let love fill us, and through that, empty us of ourselves: our preconceptions, our fears, and above all, our limited views. When we fill the bucket with fresh water, we find new trust, we combat the fear, and we widen our views because we are listening to new ideas. Our journeys must lead us to rejuvenation as often as we can. By emptying ourselves, we grow with new stems, with new energy, and with greater understanding of our purposes. Love is what empties you of yourself, but you have to allow it to prosper.

December 28

"Love is the factor that determines struggle or peace."

Love is the strongest of all the emotions. It is a connected feeling between the soul and God. It harnesses our beauty, protects our spirits, and ultimately determines our paths. When our souls and our egos are connected through love, the connectivity allows a free flow of peace and wisdom. When our souls and our egos are not connected, it causes struggle and turmoil. Love determines peace or struggle. See tomorrow's face through your actions today, and if they are in love, they will be peaceful.

December 29

"Love is the key that unlocks the soul
and leads the ego to forgetfulness."

When we soar, when we fly, we often become gripped by the passions of this world. This egotistical adventure takes us to the highest mountaintops, but it can also make us fall. Real growth comes when love unlocks the soul and the ego learns to forget itself. This rarely happens on mountaintops, but it is more evident when we search for the beauty in God. Love is the key that unlocks the soul because God is love, and when he unlocks the soul, we find that trust, faith, and belief become our companions—and we can grow in the knowledge that he knows when, how, and what we need. Love unlocks the soul—and love is God.

December 30

"Now remember this: love is precious above all things."

We must always remember—and we must always ensure that our programming reflects—that love is precious above all things. No matter who we are, what we know, or where we come from, love can overcome all. The most basic of programming functions must be to program love. And love is not the intellectual reasoning, but it is shown through practical actions. We must grow in the knowing that love is precious above all. It overcomes our fears, anxieties, and obstacles. When we are low on trust, when we are high on fear, or when we are gripped with anxiety, seek love. For love can overcome all.

December 31

"We find wisdom where we find love."

When we discover what love is, we discover our true self. We find a state where all the false facades of fear, anxiety, and pretense do not exist. Love stems directly from the soul. It sees only beauty, it knows the path, it understands wrong from right, and it clearly makes us worth much more than the ego says we are. Love in us is always divine. It knows no boundaries, gives us no limits, shows us our paths, and gives us wisdom. All it asks is that we be true, be really true, to ourselves, and therefore to love.

Epilogue

It's when we are full of wonder
when the doubt subsides,
for we feel the promise to be near.

It's then that we know
we are conquering this path.

For it's that hope, it's that belief
that allows our faith to grow.

It's then that we know.
It's then that we understand.

So, as we go, we are open to decide
for it's only when we realize that the decisions
come from the fullness of our hearts,
not through the emptiness of our minds.

Where the joy flows from,
that's the chosen path.

So, as we walk this road, seek to discover
not the empty decisions of our minds
but the fruitful flowers from our hearts.

That's the answer that brings us faith,
that makes us bold,
and eliminates the fear and anxiety.

For we are full.
Filled from within.
Not through our own making
but through the miracle from our hearts.

About the Author

K im du Preez, PhD, is a clinical psychologist who integrates her professional knowledge with deep spiritual lessons learned while walking her path to purpose. She has had to overcome challenges of infertility, adoption, and the sudden death of her husband, leaving her a single mom of two small children. Most of all, she has had to overcome the barriers of fear, anxiety, and doubt in her mind and learn to trust the beauty, wisdom, and guidance of her heart over the noise of the world.